I0310373

A MATTER
of
DISCIPLINE

―――⧫―――

By Abraham Jongroor

"Discipline thrives and is a key to success."

A Note from the Publisher

The publisher wishes to acknowledge and thank Dr Douglas H. Johnson for his invaluable help and support for Africa World Books and its mission of preserving and promoting African cultural and literary traditions and history. Dr Johnson and fellow historians have been instrumental in ensuring that African people remain connected to their past and their identity. Africa World Books is proud to carry on this mission.

© Abraham Jongroor, 2021

978-0-6451469-1-2

All rights reserved.

No part of this publication may be reproduced, stored in a retrieval system, or transmitted, in any form, or by any means, electronic, mechanical, photocopying, recording or otherwise, without the prior permission of the publishers.

This book is sold subject to the conditions that it shall not, by way of trade or otherwise, be lent, re-sold, hired out or otherwise circulated without the publisher's prior consent in any form of binding or cover other than in which it is published and without a similar condition including the condition being imposed on the subsequent purchaser.

Cover design, typesetting and layout : Africa World Books
Cover photo by jcomp / freepik

Table of Contents

Preface	v
Foreword	vii
Acknowledgements	ix
Introduction	1
My Journey	3
Step Further Away	7
Worth Risk to Take	9
Another Worthwhile Risk	13
In Somalia Territory	17
Decisiveness	20
Self-Discipline	23
Communication in General	24
Communication at Home	25
Communication and Education	26
Communication at Work	26
Communication at Public Space	27
Tolerance, Self-Respect & Self-Love	28
Body Language and Communication	29
Church Discipline - In Worship	29
Principle of Discipline in the Military	31
Body Language	31
My Second Escape	33
Humanitarian appeal	41
Alan Nichols	46
Background	47
Appeal Funds Channel	47
Follow up	51
Indiscipline Nature	52
Indiscipline	54
In Perspective	56

Preface

While I sometimes feel powerless, I know every little mark you make sends millions of waves across the family, the community, the country and the world. Self-discipline helps me to keep making those efforts! I also remember the powerful community development message of "Think global, act local". Local actions have inspired others across the world to try something similar in their own sphere/communities. I have used my life so far as an example of how to develop self-discipline and to keep working towards the greater good in complex and uncertain times.

    I start this book with an exploration of the related ideas of discipline, loyalty and respect and how those are demonstrated in good communication and the complexity of non- verbal communication cross cultures. The remainder of this book is an account of my life as a man who grew up in Sudan especially South Sudan, worked as a child in the cattle camps, gained an education including in Christian theology, fought in the resistance, moved across the world as a refugee, married and became a parent, celebrated the birth of a new nation and participated in the development of that nation with all its struggles. I have needed all courage loyalty and self-discipline I could find for that journey – which is far from over yet! I shared the good and the bad with many and my people came to know and understand me and my strong desire to contribute as a good citizen of the world.

Forword

I've written this book to help provide another perspective on the question of discipline. Please take the time to read through my accumulation of knowledge on the matter of discipline. Discipline is a broad topic which is interpreted differently by people and communities, but for me there is a common thread, a common understanding. In many, many languages the first word a child speaks is 'baba' or 'dada' and 'mama.' Teaching and providing good examples of discipline and self-discipline is one the most important tasks of parenting for both mothers and fathers because discipline especially self-discipline is a passport to success in life. Celebrities and famous people are best example because their lives are so visible to us. Understanding and communication are the keys in any relationship, and discipline – the topic of this book - in my view underpins any successful human interaction.

By putting discipline up for discussion and examination I hope I can help people who are struggling with their situations and serve to remind others who have struggled that they are not alone on their journey. It does not matter how hard the situation may be, there is still a window of hope and a chance for a success if you discipline yourself enough not be tempted by short term distractions. For everything, the time will come - good things never finish, they keep on coming!

To those who are going through difficult circumstances, be courageous, knowing that others have endured these difficulties, too and remind yourself that others have faced, and overcome, such obstacles with the right discipline. Those who have gone before and overcome, are today showing the way for others.

Acknowledgements

I want to share the people and events which have influenced me thank you all! My Mum, Athou Mach Nhial, my elder Gabriel Deng Kuol Jongroor and his friends from Yerol and Abodit invested much in me from the start of my education, in 1981. Gabriel Deng put a lot of his energy and sacrificed much of his time thinking of how to get me into school and he was the instrument to my situation of being "educated" today. Without his insistence that I attend school, I would never have achieved my current level of education.

Anything I have accomplished for South Sudan and the marginalised people of the Sudan should be attributed to the late brother Gabriel Deng Kuol Jongroor, to my father Kuol Jongroor, uncle Alier Jongroor, uncle Garang Jongroor, cousin Ayor Mabiei Jongroor, Jongroor Deng-Alish, Chuti Deng, Uncle Machar Jongroor, and Jok Akau; descendants of great grandma Adau. What a wonderful line-up in my life!

The waves of friends who been to the frontline with me during our liberation struggle for the marginalised people of South Sudan and the Sudan: Akoi Oka Riak, Garang (Malaang) Ayol, Akech Chop, Kut Anyieth, Makuach Wei Yar, Guut Agoor, Mach Guguei and many more who have engaged in our struggles. We fought without submitting to the fear in our hearts, we paid the price for the freedom of our brothers and sisters.

I acknowledge my friends from primary schools to university, teachers, and lecturers: Makuach Wei, Makuach Malek, Biar Machar, Kur Ajak, Musa, Ringdit, Nyango, Majok Mach, Wuor Dack, Machar Jongroor, Chuti Deng, Dr Charles Mphande, Annie F., Nicole, David Shires, Dr Helen Hill, etc.

I cannot leave out my friends who we went through unclear forests of Rad via Anyuak and Ethiopia: Mr. Chol Aleu, Revd. Peter Achiek, Revd. Malith Jongkuch, Mr. Nyiel Nhial, Mr. Tek Kuol, Mr. Kuot Deng, Mr. Kuol Monyjei, Mr. Ajak Akai, Mr. Ayom Ayuen Kuany, Revd. Daniel Deng Kuot and Mr. Kon Deng. Later in the "second wave" of my life as a committed person, my mother-in-law, Ms. Diing Riak; brothers-in-law Mr. Lazarus Mabiei, Mr. David Pareng; sistersin-law, Ms. Akon Manyang, Ms. Yar Anyang, Ms. Diyo Anyiway, Ms. Rebecca Anyieth, and Ms. Ayen Kuan their contributions will not go unacknowledged. You have done your bit in my second journey of my life.

Finally, and most importantly I acknowledge my beautiful, zealous, strong and intelligent wife, Mama Kuol-Mayak, Rachel Amuor Pach she is particularly special to me and to our entire family without her outstanding strength, I would have not accomplished what I had accomplished in Australia today.

Introduction

This book is about sharing my experience in fields of discipline in a minimal form in all areas I lived, worked and still pushing me. Especially Self-discipline is my life propeller. This book will discuss a lot about how discipline helped me and how it may shape your life for the matter as you progress in your field of dreams and relationships.

The world does not work in our favour all the time, but we should not allow it to divert our directions. It may support us for a short while, or it may favour our lives with a long run of good luck. It provides all your needs for your life and for future generations. I call this "turnaround from God,' from our Creator who gives and takes. Discipline especially self-discipline is a powerful weapon of success and this what I am sharing with you here in this book.

Discipline matters and it is a passport to success. God commanded his people in the Ten Commandments to, "Honour your father and your mother, that your days may be long upon the land which the Lord, your God is giving you," (Ex 20: 1 – 17). This Bible verses are the fundamental principle of self-discipline. This is a call for discipline! Discipline is the pathway to every meaningful thing in life, to all achievement, both public and private. Without discipline there is no respect; without respect there is no order and peace. These things work hand in hand. When discussing the relationship between parents and their children, wife and husband, boss and staffs we do need to reflect on the wisdom - "those who love (their children) ……are careful to discipline them," (Prov. 13:24).

A MATTER OF DISCIPLINE

I think that discipline is a responsibility, a mark of respect, an accountability, a standard of loyalty and ultimately a privilege to let you reach your potential. When a person is undisciplined, they do not fulfil their duties in a visible and satisfactory manner and perhaps do not fulfil their potential. Loyalty and discipline together work to achieve worthwhile outcomes. Loyalty is an unwavering commitment to your people, your conscience, your country and your culture. Today many countries and many communities are unstable primarily because of lack of discipline and loyalty. The absence of loyalty goes hand in hand with a deep disrespect which can spread like a plague through the nation and this social dis-ease brings about anxiety, outrage, and unrest in the populace. Public servants who have loyalty to their county display the discipline to declare any conflict of interest before they are appointed or elected. This transparent mindset is critical for fair and proper administration.

Discipline demonstrates care, shows ongoing commitment and sustains the well-being of both the individual and the community. Discipline supports confidence and confidence is a common attribute of successful people. Self-disciplined people are leaders in their own rights. They have a clear vision, a visible mission and purpose and so are filled with confidence to achieve their goals.

Discipline of the self is the dominating principle. If people do not apply discipline to themselves (self-discipline), they will fail to achieve their dreams. Everywhere peoples' heads are filled with dreams, but the dreams just remain dreams, nothing is achieved, because they lack the discipline to activate those dreams, to turn them into reality. I have researched many successful people and read their testimonies; discipline is a common characteristic of success.

Everybody knows the complexity of the idea of discipline. I have found it useful to investigate other people's perspectives. John Maxwell, my favourite leadership author says, the reason he writes books is to communicate with millions of people at once. He likes communicating to people to give them a chance of reflecting on their daily life and to keep things firmly in context and perspective.

Let us pause and take a moment to define discipline. It is defined as, *the practice of training people to obey rules or a code of behaviour, using punishment to correct disobedience. And the practice of exercising self-regulation. (Oxford English dictionary 2004)* All institutions, both public and private, have distinctive disciplines, codes of behaviour, which are practiced, or at least aspired to be practiced.

The origin of this word/term and meaning: It originates from the Latin, 'discipulus,' meaning instruction, knowledge. Currently this term is used differently in many ways, it can be by physical punishment, teaching, suffering or martyrdom, this can be branched into several classifications as school discipline, military discipline, police discipline, court discipline among others and so forth.

Therefore, this book discussed all these & specified them in individual mindedness so that we relate them and reflect how they can reset our paths and never let go the opportunity.

My Journey

I am a child who grew up in a patriarchal society with my siblings. We were looked after by our single mother who (lost her husband in her mid-30s). My dad was a good man according to his colleagues and friends. My dad, Kuol Jongroor was the 2nd among his 19 maternal siblings to die in his late thirties in intercommunal fighting in January 1968.

My mum is a tough and resilient single mother who knows how to look after herself and her family. Mum sacrificed her womanhood, the prime years of her adult life and her personal desires for her children. I always think of her courage, self-discipline and resilience. I think of her singlemindedness and unlimited caring to do what she did for her family, the family of Kuol Jongroor the family of Athou Mach Nhial. God blesses her.

Despite Mum being head of the house, she had to consult with her brothers – in - law who were like caretakers of us before anything could happen. To remain a loyal wife of the family she must abide by family rules of submissiveness and togetherness. In this way education in my family was a secondary thing, not valued much, therefore it was treated by them just like nothing. School was where less active children were sent so that they can support themselves in later life. No one really knew what value education brings to the family since it was not encouraged enough by the government of the time. The thing that was well known to us from those children sent to school was spending. When they return home, they just come looking for a cow, goat or sheep to sell in order to buy all school materials, which makes it difficult for families like ours to cope. It was not considered as a thing of value or as an investment in the future. The important things in most adult lives were land and cattle. Those made sense to them. As a result, active kids were considered as most valuable to the family, useful to make the family prosper from land and cattle. I was among those active kids in our family so my uncles saw me as a potential person who would one day benefit the family like most families in our community.

I am the 5th in line of 8 children and the 4th boy inline of sonhood in the family and the 3rd of the 8 children to attend school. To attend school was considered unusual in my childhood by my uncle Deng Jongroor and I believe it was the same among other families. The reason was that 2 consecutive sons should not go to school just like that. We were fatherless in first place which made attending school even more difficult in a patriarchal society like our community. On the other hand, my 2nd elder brother Gabriel Deng Kuol was among first kids to attend school in 1973 after the Addis Ababa agreement between Anyanya I (Southern Sudan rebel) and the Sudan government, perhaps the generation to break the cycle of consecutive brothers/siblings to join school. This places me in a second position of responsibility in the family rural setup. My brother Gabriel Deng worked very hard to make it possible for me to attend school by any means possible. We love each other very much; we were not like younger and elder brothers.

As an active boy who grew up among nomadic young men who roamed far, far away from rest of our community to graze their cattle, I was required to work harder. Mostly we survived only on milk, with no meat and no traditional cereal food to balance the diet. I had to be creative to keep myself and those young men healthy and strong. As such, I used to go to nearby communities and exchange my milk with either groundnuts (peanuts), maize or sorghum. This was to make up for them to be strong enough to be able to face external threats.

Anything needs a push; it needs somebody to push you from behind or to tap your shoulder. Gabriel Deng Kuol tried everything to make me realise my potential if I am educated and fulfill his dream that one day, we would be performing together in intellectual world work side by side, supporting each other and realising our achievement together. He was a dedicated, disciplined young man. His foresight and tenacity opened many opportunities for everyone in our family.

My elder brother, Gabriel Deng Kuol, was sent to school in May 1973 after the Addis Ababa agreement of 1972, with the southern Sudanese rebels (1956 – 1972) known as Anyanya I. This was the first Sudanese civil war. He encouraged me to join him in school at all cost, which I resisted for several reasons for years, with the support of my uncle, Deng Jongroor, who preferred me to mind our cattle, at least until my younger brother, Akau Kuol, joined Deng in school in 1977. Akau was less active that made my uncle Deng Jongroor comfortable to send him to school. I was very, very active looking after the cattle and everyone in our family, and that convinced my uncle Deng Jongroor not to release me for duties other than minding cattle-herding. Looking after our cattle was essential to him because the cattle were our only livelihood we had, without this kind of economic security, we would be just liability to them as uncles. Seven fatherless boys would be a huge burden on him when they grow up. We were also hard to support in terms of getting married in the Jieng tradition, doweries and families' establishment thereafter. Who could afford to pay the bride prices for 7 boys with only one sister? We also have step siblings who also require a huge support because they were also young. Strategically and economically his thinking was logical as someone in charge and head of liability. My brother Deng Kuol thought our uncle Deng Jongroor was wrong in his thinking, different perspective at different world' levels. My brother had no choice but to listen to our uncle and do what he was told. But, being a disciplined boy, Deng Kuol never gave up on his mission to bring me, Abraham to school with him. It might have seemed that uncle Deng was playing a tricky game by saying "we can't let Gabriel and Abraham who are younger and elder brothers go to school. We have to skip Abraham and take Akau instead." This unclear principle made Gabriel so sceptical of our uncle motive because uncle Deng didn't implement his thinking with his own sons, so why us! Deng Kuol doubted the motives of our uncle, Deng Jongroor.

Gabriel Deng kept pushing with his mission, taking me to school. Finally, in May 1981, his plans fell in place. All was good, including at last, the opportunity to relax a little. There was no more pressure from those older cousins and my uncles, no more bullying or coercion.

One evening Deng Kuol arrived at the cattle camp site of Angana, Juba. He was there looking for me to go to Juba then to Bor so that I could attend school. He circumvented everyone including my uncles and cousins and there was no means of communication except by a messenger on foot. Deng strongly believed in me, he believed that one day we would do things better together, as one unit and on the same side not like our uncles (educated & uneducated). I was in awe of his planning which was very smart. When I arrived from the bush with the news that I had killed two warthogs and that I needed people to go and fetch them, I found Deng Kuol and he said, "I need you; we are leaving tomorrow morning because our mum is so sick and soon no one will be looking after her since Akau and I are going to school in three weeks and you know that every crop season is a bad time for our mom." This is the time when she gets sick and if there is no one to look after her, there will be no harvest and her life also will be in danger." He went on and on with many convincing words and arguments. After lengthy discussion between us, our uncle, Angok Ajiu

Mach, joined in till almost daybreak before others joined in, working hard to persuade me. Off we went in the morning on the journey to Juba. In the afternoon we arrived and went straight to the market to buy school uniforms. He measured them on me and when I asked him why he measured them on me he replied that Akau was the same size as yourself. So, I thought they were for Akau and I was ignorant of his motives. Still heading on our journey, we went to the truck station, aiming to travel to Bor next morning. With his friends we got a truck leaving for Bor at 7AM in morning, still not knowing what was happening. If my cousins and uncles had been aware of what was going to happen, they wouldn't have let me go with him. This was the end of my being used at the cattle camp as provider. I was going for something bigger for this family (Dengalish). Today is a live witness.

Step Further Away

As journey (development) continued, we become even a bit aware of our national politics, we began to be something else. On May 16th 1983 after 3 years of my primary education though I skipped that level, war broke out again. This was the Sudan 2nd civil war, instigated by officers of the Sudanese army forces base in Bor and that was the birth of the Sudanese People's Liberation Army/Movement (SPLA/M). This was the second phase of my life's journey and the most dangerous of all. Everything was affected including my education, especially in Bor District where the movement was strong, there were no classes. My brother and I decided to join the movement. Deng Kuol joined in Sept. 1983 and in December I followed him. This was another journey, another mission to provide to others in need of a big shift, a change of governance system and the recognition of equal citizenry for all Sudanese people regardless of their race and religion.

This mission took me to Ethiopia where I was still caring for my young cousins who joined the SPLA/M together with me. It was tough and so difficult to imagine that an 18-year-old was looking after 16- & 17-years old boys on a journey to such a wild environment. Joining the movement was a good thing for me to have done despite all the losses including cousins and brother Deng.

In May – Sept 1984 in Bonga military training centre in Ethiopia, we used to have a motto so that we could accomplish any task imposed on us by the trainers, whether the task was a punishment or duty of the day, we sang. *'Këriëc ëbën ee ya tɔŋ, wanë thïn yala, ye nut, ye gedem, ye koor, ye jebel yala'* (Everything is a battle, take it on straight). According to D. Prayer, 'Happiness is dependent on self-discipline. We are the biggest obstacles to our own happiness". Not everybody made it to the finish line with our training at Bonga military training centre. Few comrades died during those activities, but those who made it are now enjoying the fruit of their effort and sacrifice in the Republic of South Sudan as a proud independent nation since 2006. However, it is not without a cost inflicted on us by our own sons.

As part of furthering away from home. I arrived in Australia as a refugee in 2002. Here I started a new life, and in 2005 I proudly became an Australian citizen, the new home. People are created differently in the way they see and do things. I prefer to work for the benefit of others. I feel better when I see others getting ahead and prospering, especially my family, friends and community at large that is why I studied community development. I am the 5th child in family of 8 children and all of us, despite being fatherless, were brought up according to the Jieng (Dinka) culture and norms (socialists in nature) share every little you have. We do a lot to support rest of our extended families and we expect nothing in return. This approach is ingrained in my personality, no matter what the price to myself. My wife is the same. We share the values of generosity and community interest. Our mothers taught us those important values.

When I joined the Sudan People Liberation Army/Movement (SPLA/M) in 1983 it was not something I thought would last for long. It was just a matter of time and our people would be liberated, the people who were like refugees in their own land. You will read more about what I feel about where my people and I belong. There is nowhere I feel more like being known because of my abilities and intelligence. This is now our big challenge in South Sudan. We see ourselves as distinct and separate tribes not as individuals to be taken on merit, and not as people of one nation called South Sudan.

Worth Risk to Take

Anybody can claim it to have seen all, but with different experiences. It could be bad or it could be awe depend on individual circumstances even those who have seen nothing can claim it.

It happened after Dr Riek Machar rebellion against movement the SPLM in 1991. It was seen by wise/nationalists as rebellion against leadership of Dr John Garang, the leader of Sudan People Liberation Movement/Army (SPLM/A), but it was not. It was not that way. It turned out differently, it was rebellion against any tribe in Sudan who were fighting against regime in Khartoum particularly Jieng Bor. How do we define this? A puppet of Khartoum, he turned out be. It happened that everyone who happens not to be from Nuer tribe should be killed in exception of Cholo of Dr Lam Akol, the traitor of larger tribe in South Sudan.

We all claimed it to have lost our sons, daughters and properties, but there are those who bear it most and paralysed/crippled families to the point of no quick recovery or no return at all.

Bor District is one of the communities most affected and has never recovered till today. After Riek Machar forces (Nuer Militia) completed their mission of killing all SPLA officers in whole of Upper Nile region as his zone as zonal commander of Movement, he mobilised his cousins to attack Bor, Pariang, Korpulus and many more in Upper Nile region. He succeeded so much in Bor because all capable Bor's sons were everywhere in Sudan as fighting force for the movement in which majority of them were slaughtered in Upper Nile region particularly in Nasir, Laar and unity state. Riek forces cleaned up Bor and looted all their properties, abducting women, girls, children and massacre most. Millions of cattle were taken to Nuer land with little resistance. Kuol Manyang who was a zonal commander was around Juba with number of commanders including Dr. John Garang and William Nyuon Beny. The reason of them all being there was to capture Juba, the capital of the South Sudan and ready to declare total Victory of liberation of South and declare autonomous government and making Juba a seat of New Sudan vision, which was later aborted. Kuol Manyang and other commanders were asked to ease Juba siege and started campaign against Dr Riek forces starting from Mangala to where they came from.

Dr. Riek instead of fighting for the cost of marginalised people of Sudan, he became a South Sudanese back stabber. He drove off all survivors from Bor and follow them toward Juba where SPLA forces were in a pierce fighting with Sudan army over the control of the city. But Dr. Riek intention was in opposite, stop SPLA from capturing the city. In that sense, he succeeded, SPLA back off from capturing Juba and turned against him. All lives lost in Juba and resources used went in vain. None had benefit from that between Riek and SPLA/M mainstream, but enemy, the Khartoum regime. Juba was saved by their puppet.

It will look naïve to claim it myself that I have seen it all, the bad and good. However, there is a sense of it. I didn't live with my dad long enough nor with my mom; I had seen none of my grandparents from both sides of my mum and my dad. My dad got killed while I was 2 - 3 years old and I believe, because I am still able to remember few belongings of my dad. The things he used to do to us every morning and the day our beads/ necklace were removed in April 1968 which is traditionally sign of grieving for loss of loves ones. 2 - 3years of my whole life that only I spent with my dad and after that my childhood changed terribly and gloomy without dad nor grandparents. Not only that the whole of my life was so chartered. Parents plan future of their children together, but only person who used to sleep and think about us was our mum, the rock of our family. Till now I feel shame to use traditionally honorary call of 'baba' dad or 'kuarkuar' grandpa or 'koko' grandma because I am not use to any. I lost them all, to get use of these honorary now is to name my kids after them so that I start practice what I lost during my childhood otherwise. Grandparents are catalyse while parents are silver head of the family.

I know number of other kids in my community who lived the same life, but I don't think they lived the same way I did at certain level. I got only one auntie, Akuol Mach Nhial from my mum side who also lost everything including her off springs and husband.

Traditionally in our culture, your aunt is like your mum and her kids are like your siblings, but I (we) had none. What should I (we) claim to have enjoyed personally in the World that I had childhood? Nothing, but my life, my mum's strength and courage still provides us sanctuary.

As my teenage came about, it was also a bad time. I went through drainage of lifetime. My brother, the one I look up to, the boy I love most Gabriel Deng Kuol joined school and left me at village/cattle herding lifestyle, they are totally different lifestyle all together. I was totally lost in a sense and was beyond his capacity as a boy who lost his dad in early age in a patriarchal society. As we grew up in a completely different world, town and village. He insisted secretly in his heart behind our uncles that we should not live in separate/different lifestyle.

He gave me an example in our family, my uncles don't enjoy their time together with uncle Machar Jongroor, their own brother. He always leaves them as soon as his colleagues come for a visit. He must go to his colleagues leaving his brothers lingering by themselves. In his (Gabriel) heart and mind he doesn't like to see that happen between us two. In April 1981 he came to collect me to join him in school but approach it indirectly due to his experienced from previous attempts. Unfortunately, we are never last long. Exactly 5 years later (April 1981 – April 1986) he left the world as my hero & our hero because he died in battlefield of Kurmuk as martyr. Instead of saying let's go to school, he tricked me and everybody else, especially uncle Angok Ajiu. He said our mum is so sick and this time is time of cultivation and I am now going to go to school and there will be no one to look after her. I refused because it was a high time of my later teen- hood and life was under my control base on what I envisioned in that World of ours, rural lifestyle. Every requirement of life was under my palm such as wrestling, hunting, zeal of providing including protection of property in that World. There I went with him, after a quite intense discussions and heart felt touches. After I joined school, we were still apart in term of school setting. He was in secondary boarding school in the City (Mading) and I was in primary boarding school in the village (kapat). We were still unable to regularly meet though the places where not that fare from each other, the distance between the two was about 16km. After three years in school, the distance expanded, he joined the movement (SPLM/A) leaving me behind. Would it not been him, I might had made wrong choice.

All these unfortunate transactions indeed separated us more and forever. Early Sept. 1983, he left Bor with some of our cousins, then later at the end of Dec 1983 after 5 months, I started my own journey with some other cousins. When we arrived in Ethiopia in Early Feb 1984, we still couldn't meet. He was at his final Military Intelligence (MI) training in Addis Ababa while we were still in refugee camp before we could attend our military training at Bonga. 2 months later, we went for our military training, luckily enough he was informed about my arrival at the site but wasn't sure of who of his brothers arrived. With his keen and knowledge of me, he concluded in his mind that it was me who had made it, so he bought me so tracksuits to assist me during training as we were having no clothes left on us. Most of our (Chol Machar, Madul Garang, Makuach Wei & I) clothes were sold for food in last two months when we were in refugee camp. After one month at military training camp, Gabriel graduated and directly deployed at our camp as head of intelligent officers placed on various battalions.

In this journey, none of us was certainly sure of what was going to happen to each of us in individual space or circumstances of struggle.

I was not thinking of going joining the movement. I was okay to go back to my world, the cattle camp to herd our cattle. Suddenly in

December 1983 I changed my plan and thought why not I shouldn't join the SPLM/A, then off I went. It took us at least two months to reach Achua (Itang) through hardship. We walk day and night because of fear of Nuer militia, Anyanya II, instead of fighting our common enemy, the Khartoum government they turn against their fellow brothers in liberation.

What did we benefit here? We lost everything including lives and '*Aŋuem*' as Dr. John Garang once said, but we are still rich. "I am rich, but not with money, I am rich in culture and its legacy that I carry and my grandkids will carry" aborigines woman said. (Dianne Kerr). Indeed, we have our freedom and pride which our grandkids will be carrying forever. Discipline was our spirit that made us carry on in those hardship. Our dream was that one day we will be free forever.

According to Dianne, we have stories from each other, understand each other and live-in harmony.

Why does discipline, especially self-discipline, matter? It makes us set the right priorities for ourselves and our surrounding environment. When we are not disciplined, we mess those priorities without right direction and wander like untamed animals in the wilderness of society.

Indiscipline is a sickness by itself, it is like a mental disorder. It makes us odd among our peers, behaviourally and approach-wise. It is a fraction of bad feeling and envying. It also makes us jealous about others; it controls us to the point that we like gossiping aiming of assassinating others' character.

Another Worthwhile Risk

In July 1995 I took another risk after successful completion of my high school in Ethiopian and go through the most dangerous Somalia at the time aiming at reaching Kenya from the East as we failed to gain access from the North (Ethiopian – Kenya border). It was another hard decision to make as there was no other way, I could imagine to possibly help my community the way I want in future if I remain in Ethiopia. Helping others was my goal.

Individually, there was no problem as I was assistance to Anglican Minister of St Mathew parish in Addis Ababa, capital of Ethiopia. I was offered a place at Evangelical Theological College in Addis Ababa even before my national exam's results were out with condition that if "I could get 'C' grade in English" in National results. When my results came out, my English Grade was even higher 'B' Grade which guarantee further studies. I was between 6th & 7th, will I go for Theology degree or go for resettlement in US, Canada, or Australia! It was a tough choice in hand. We are always face with tough choices and must weigh between individual benefits and compound (us) benefits. It was the same scenario which faced us at Pakok temporary settlement camp in South Sudan territory after we (Sudanese Refugees) were dislodged from Ethiopia in May 1991. Because of its magnitude impact in my future and my friendship with colleagues, I must consult them first, especially Daniel Deng Kuot in US and Chol Aleu in Jima, Ethiopia of what should I do about this. They were the only people in my reach at the time. At this stage Malith Jongkuch and Peter Achiek were already in Kenya and was no way to reach them. None of us were having phone or mailing details especially Malith & Peter. I was able to send mails to Deng in USA and vice versa. The decision was tough and decisive. I should go to Refugee camp in Kenya, but through tough terrain. It was unthinkable attempt to take a flight to Kenya. I have no kind of identification document like birth certificate, passport, even UNHCR card which may help me to think of air ticket. Then the only option I was left with was to go through illegal mean. Though there was no document on me, I must stick to my old plan because Kenya was the only country in the region where resettlement processes were available for everyone. The illegal mean was to go footing through border as a refugee or asylum seeker. It is the only way I could possibly make it, but I should first inform parish Vicar who was working hard for me to get me a scholarship and many other things because I do not want to offend him. I was in a difficult position, but I must face him since tomorrow is mine. I went to him courageously in the office. I said to him, look here Minister I am faced with a situation and I know it is not a right decision, but I have considered it to be necessary. I have decided, I am leaving for Kenya and the aim is to go and look for an opportunity of resettlement in one of OECD Countries. It was like striking of electricity shock on his brain. He (Minister) went cold for few minutes; I am sure he was sorting & weighing all options in his mind. After few minutes of silent, he raised his head and called me "Abraham it is your own will, but not God will". I was well prepared because I know how closely I was working with him in term of working with most asylum seekers in Addis Ababa. Again, I took few deep breaths then responded to him, look I am from a large family and I will be only person in the family with Degree what will I do with it? I will help nobody of this family, and I am sure if I manage to go for resettlement, I will be able to assist at least 30+ people in this family and that will help me by giving me peace of mind that I have fulfilled my duty in the family. There is nothing that will make me happy than making this family happy again after many loses in War of Liberation in South Sudan. Because of these situations I am leaving sorry, then I left. The lives I have changed now is more than 30 persons, that figure is not even $1/5^{th}$ of lives I have changed whether direct or indirect.

I did this not because I knew what was going to happen to us on the way between Kenyan - Ethiopian border but believe that my team and I will make it to where we want to go. First challenge was issue of money, second obstacle was documents (ID) for me and few others and last challenge was route to take due to insecurity all along the way. All of these were not easy to think about. The thing that came to mine was let's use what we have and when it finishes that will be it. We must take risks since we are leaving no wives or children behind. Off we went to the border at separate trips. After we assembled at border town of Moyale Ethiopia we prepare early entry to Kenya, the battle of survival began (July 1995), it was like ground-breaking game or D

– Day Landings of 6th June 1944 of Allied forces invasion of Normandy town, France. Early in the morning we crossed the border into Kenya, holding on with Kenyan police was exactly like military invasion. We were set down and guarded by few numbers of police officers while authority was busy mobilising dozens more from the region especially riot police. They were pretending to be working with us and have called UNHCR agent in the region so that they can come and register us while in fact they were working on their contingency plan. After they gathered quite large number of riot police, they surrounded us at midday and started beating us, teargassing us and tried to pull us apart. We tried our best to remain stick together and help ourselves by watering ourselves so that teargas could harm us not. It was tougher than we anticipated. After 12pm we were all exhausted and police began to pull us apart one by one then started throwing us into the river like dead bodies, but luckily enough, there was a very tiny strip island which none of the two countries (Ethiopia and Kenya) could bother to get us off. After two days on that island water began to rise because it was a rainy season and dry place began to narrow and narrow in addition to luck of shelters. In addition, it was not only the water that was threatening us on the land strip (island); armed bandits and food were other stand by enemies in silent. In the evening, we set and discussed of what would be an end to this waiting on this piece of land. Some of us were arguing that let's remain here till UNHCR protection staffs arrive and some of us including myself were sceptical of UN visit. The question I asked people was so simple. Who will let UN know that we are here? Ethiopia will not and Kenya will not since they removed us from their mainland. The meeting ended without conclusion, then cracks in the group started. So, some group members in the night came to me after they come back to their senses and began to explore my idea and I told them look here we are at no man land how long are we going to be here and what will happen next if UNHCR do not come. My thinking at the time was to go back to Moyale – Ethiopia and in the morning, we should go to Somalia and there we may be able to go to Kenya through Somalia. The name Somalia was like poison in a food because it was a year Bush the senior withdrew US Forces in Somalia and country was a country without government and worse of it, they do not like to see any Christian entering their country because they are potential enemies of Islam. I told them look there are always opportunities in a circumstance like this, let us turn lack of government in Somali into opportunity. They all went away except 3 guys, William Deng Mayom – currently in Australia, Aban Ayul Anyui – currently in South Sudan and Amum Malual Machar – currently in USA. They told me let us try your idea. Without wasting of time, we immediately left the group of more than 30 people. As soon as we left that island, bandits struck and took every belonging and number of people sustained injuries. That was the end of dream of crossing border to Kenya through Moyale for those whom we left behind there.

In Somalia Territory

At midday we took off from Ethiopian border town aiming to reach Ethiopian – Somalia border Southeast region. That journey took us about 3 hours to arrive at our designated destination. Things went as predicted, no one stopped us from crossing into the country. Without wasting time, we proceeded to border town of Moyale from Somalia border. We were lucky enough to meet a Somali returnee from USA who symphysis with our situation, he took us to other side of the border (Kenya) immediately and negotiated on our behalf with Kenyan authority and all ended in vain. We were rejected. He returned to Somalia with us because there was no other option left though he was under pressure from his group of not to keep us, but to kill us instead "we are waste". The reason was simple, we are Christian and therefore we are brothers to American who destroyed their country in last 2 years (1992 – 1993) of their present in there (Somalia). They did not see us as African brothers, too they did not see us as brothers from Horn of Africa, think on religion base enmity.

Zu – 23 Anti-Aircraft

Returning to Somalia with us was not his choice, but there was nothing else he could possibly do to help us in his humanity feeling. We could observe his body language that something is not right. We do not understand what others were saying to him, but his face expression communicates something to us. It was a **nightmare, I tell you**. Everything that come after our returned was not our expectation. We were placed in a three bedrooms house that was used as store of food and ammunition. It was heavily guard with four antiaircraft machine guns (Zu 23), the Soviet made, one at each corner of the building.

It was a tough moment; however, our moral, communication and belief kept our resilience alive throughout that night. I made myself clear to brothers not to say anything stupid, something that may attract more questions which we may not be in position to answer in a convincing way. If we talk much, we may directly or indirectly offend them and may put our lives more at risk at most. I was very keen in angle and I was the only most experienced person among them in term of military intelligent when it comes to interrogation. First, we were caught off guard in the sense of individual's interrogation. Luckily enough I was the first to be called in, none of us was aware of the motive of calling us out individually. We were only prepared to be interviewed as a group. Fortunately, my orientation from the beginning when we entered Somalia was well kept in mind of everyone. "Don't panic, don't say too much, be precise, say I don't understand if you want to, stand your ground on your belief (religion), etc.". When I was taken in, three of my colleagues were left like a sheep without shepherd so then they quickly met and discussed what they could do in possibility of bad outcomes and for most the death. What will they do if I am not coming back? However, they never shown sign of panicking or wobbling. They remained calm and firm with the mood we entered Somalia. To convince these brothers (Somali boys) we must explain it to them that this is the only route we could possibly reach Kenya and we need your help. Nothing will change that fact. The guy (commander) who is supporting us will have enough ammunition to fight back against those who are after our lives. Even if it comes to worse scenario of death, let it be. Sometimes things are planned by creator before we are born. Our fate is already determined at this stage and we cannot change the outcome. Fortunately, we were having an asset among us, William Deng. William was a qualified Islamic teacher; he was a Quran teacher when he was in Khartoum and he knows how to recite Quran from beginning to the end. The room we were taken into was so scary to begin with. It was so dark, so scary making the night even so gloomy, darker and longer. They setup a separate room where they call us in one by one. The serious thing that made it even too frightening was that when they took one of us out of the room, they don't take us back in the same room we were. They put those of us who finished interrogation together in a separate room. What would come to your mind in this situation if you happened to be the one left behind and to be call in next? Got killed right? That was a conclusion in every single of us mind, but for me it was nothing new. Death is always one way which we may not escape from when it comes. I was not like other colleagues because I was the first to attend the interview, but my colleagues were in the state of anguish and weariness. The second person who followed me was so relieved after he met me after his interrogation. We hugged each other as we had never made for long time then he narrated their feelings after I left them in the room. The reason he was so relief was that, Since I am still alive there will be nothing danger happening to us again though we were still under confinement. Then the third and fourth persons followed. It was a joyous and happiness moment like we were separated for so many years though uncertainty was still awaiting us.

Since there was no head way in this border town, we opted to go deep further into Somalia which was our original plan. We must go through Mogadishu, the Somalia Capital and from there we will come to Kenya through Garissa border town from the East with believe that Kenyan police may allow us through in sympathy. However, question of insecurity remains a concern. This Somali guy who took us to Kenya at Moyale met us after interviews and advised us to go the way we choose, but fear of land mines and warlords in Jubba region; however, he wishes us a good luck. We were spared and he assured us that if he is still in charge of Moyale Somalia border force, there will be nothing bad happening to us. We spent night under serious and heavy security. Though we perceived those who were guarding us as our potential threat, but in opposite, they looked after us till morning. Public outside there were our worse enemies.

In the morning, he came to pick us up and drop us somewhere safe outside far away from the town using his guards as passengers so that we look like people on a mission. Our car was full of his men. His intention was to put public opinion that we are being taken away for an execution outside the town so that they stop attacking us. His assumption didn't work as he thought. As soon as we boarded the vehicle and started driving away, we found ourselves in hail of stones everywhere with shouts in the Somali language which we couldn't understand and people kept coming out of the houses along the streets as driver tried his best to get us away as fast as he could to avoid this storm of stones. He then geared off the road and drove through suburbs to avoid contact with many people who were just rushing toward the road ahead of us. In the end, he managed to drive us out safely. Through the forest, we managed to join the road. He was mainly fearing of landmine in the surrounding off road. Somali warlords planted a lot of landmines everywhere during civil war and during their war with United State lead humanitarian intervention force from 1992 – 1993, luckily enough there were no mines where we drove.

Self-discipline is a consistency, patience, and resilience in life. All successful people in all fields possess self-discipline at most. It is the last character they could lose in their lives. Consistency, determination and believe as elements of self-discipline safeguard our mission.

Decisiveness

Right-set discipline helps us in number of forms. We view it in different angles depend on what we face or envisage for ourselves and society we live in.

"Believe in yourself, and the rest will fall into place. Have faith in your own abilities, the hard work and there is nothing you cannot accomplish." Brad Henry. Isn't this enlighten us of how we could look at discipline at this angle? Discipline doesn't come and applied itself, but it is accompanied by variety of things starting with you as a person, believe in your ability and hard work. Many people call me with names they choose based on time they had with me, either unhappy with me or happy with me and this could be situational.

When we went back to Ethiopia in Sept 1991 after Riek Machar and Lam Akol declared their rebellion against Dr. John Garang in Sudan Liberation Army/Movement, we were not sure of what will happen to us either on the way or within Ethiopia when we arrive there; however, one thing was certain, we will get back to the school and one day we will have our degrees because we first believe in ourselves. We were having confidence in ourselves; we were like Israelite leprosy sufferers who decided to go to Aramean's camp (2Kings 7: 3 -11). They talked to themselves of either die or live (the City of

Samara was besieged by Aramean's forces for long time till there was no food left for people to eat in the City. It was a city without hope, a dead city, but their Lord God said don't lose hope I will reinstate you...). Our inner discipline and voices within us were telling us look, nothing terrible will happen to you and your belief is guaranteed. In fact, we went through enormous challenges on our way, but in the end, we reached our destination without life lose. After reaching Ethiopia even after we settled into Ethiopian Education system through United Nation High Commission for Refugees (UNHCR) we were still facing challenges like what faced us in our journey from Sudan to Ethiopia. On our way we were at direct risk of death from Ethiopian soldiers, wild animals like Ethiopian Bear and Anyuak community before reaching camp manages by UNHCR. Our Nuer brothers who were with us in the school become even difficult to manage because there were large number of them, and we were minority amidst. Dr. Riek and Dr. Lam split from mainstream SPLA/M and formed so-called Nasir faction of the SPLA/M which later transform itself into South Sudan Independent Movement (SSIM). They constantly threat us with death. Some of us were filled with discontent and high tension of declaring conflict within school which few of us managed to defuse, however fighting did happen in Dimma Refugee Camp were one of our brothers Ayom Ayuen Kuany got killed. How did we defused the situation from getting out of hand was our inner self-discipline? We knew why we were there. We convinced some of our brothers who were totally outraged by behaviours by reminding them the reason which led us to Ethiopia. The reason we came here is other than fighting anybody, but to get education, our opponents are hopeless their academic performances were self-evidence. We believe in ourselves first and rest fall in place. What we envisaged was achieved 23 years later, all of us are now university graduates. Among my peers I was the last to settle in Australia after11 years. Revd. Daniel Deng went to USA (1994), Revd. Peter John and Revd. Jacob Malith went to Canada (2000 & 2001 respectively) Chol Aleu (1997) and I settled in Australia (2002). "Believe in yourself! Have faith in your abilities! Without a humble but reasonable confidence in your own powers you cannot be successful or happy." Norman Vincent Peale.

Do you believe this? Yes, I do. Belief (acceptance) and faith (trust) have almost similar meaning; however, play slightly different roles in context of our journey of life determination.

The bush of South Sudan – Ethiopia border was so wild, day was not safe (human threat), and night wasn't safe either (wild animal) but no one among us was thinking much about those threats. In us was determination, faith and believe. We were certain that something will come out of this struggle. The most threatening was human than wild animals. We said to ourselves, with our bare hands we can fight off animals, but we can't withstand human (guns) with our bare hands. So, we decided to walk at night and hide during the day to avoid encountering human. However, assumptions are not always accurate. One night at round 4am on 10th Sept 199, I will never forget that morning. We accidentally felt into Uyane's (Ethiopian rebel) ambush. They were made alert by our first group (Malith, Deng & Chol) who passed before our second group could approach that location. Luckily, they were not the main enemy we fear most. "Success is no accident. It comes because of hard work, perseverance, learning, studying, sacrifice and most of all, love of what you are doing or learning to do." Pele. "Work hard for what you want because it won't come to you without a fight. You must be strong and courageous and know that you can do anything you put your mind to. If somebody puts you down or criticizes you, just keep on believing in yourself and turn it into something positive." Leah LaBelle.

Self-Discipline as a Better Alternative to External Discipline

Self-discipline is what it takes to live a rewarding life and it starts with self-respect, the first step towards self-discipline. Respect your efforts, respect yourself, Self- respect leads to self-discipline. When we have both firmly under your belt, that's real power and this is what we must understand.

Buddha once said; "To enjoy good health, to bring happiness to one's family, to bring peace to all, one must first discipline and control one's own mind. If a man can control his mind, he can find the way to Enlightenment, and all wisdom and virtue will naturally come to him."

G. R. Blair states it clearly in quote, 'Self-discipline is an act of cultivation.' As with growing a crop, it will take time to produce a tangible result. If you are kind of person who does not like to wait for tomorrow, it is hard for you to harvest any result. It requires you to connect today's actions to tomorrow's results. It makes us think of the proverb in the Bible that says, there is a time for everything. "There is a season for sowing, a season for reaping" – (Ecclesiasts 3:1). Self-discipline helps you know which is which." You and I must have the patience to see the result of our investment. Why is it important to have self-discipline as a foundation? Is it because when you associate yourself with self-discipline, almost anything is possible?

Being disciplined by others discipline is not pleasant. It is so painful or humiliating when applies on to you by 2nd or a 3rd party and for this reason, I'd rather apply it onto myself than have it applied onto me by someone else like being taken to court by complainant or jail and guarded by authority. Finding oneself in prison/jail is like discipline being enforced by 3rd party. If you could had applied it against yourself a long time ago, it would have not reached to that lockdown which isolates you from family, friends, and productivity.

I believe being disciplined is very intimidating when you hear it from someone else. Lacking discipline, need some discipline measures, disciplinary steps, it touches our emotions and distorts our thinking ability. The other downturns of re-enforced discipline by authority includes being recorded in public database, deprives us from accessing our dream careers.

So, disciplining oneself is preferable because it guarantees amount of values of respect in society.

Applying discipline onto yourself is a better, cheapest, very practical, and easy way. When we go to school we are taught, nurtured to maturity by teachers and the education system then when we are matured enough in the system of education, we decide which discipline or route we would take. You will choose a path into higher education according to your interest; you choose the *discipulus* and the faculty.

"Discipline is the bridge between goals and accomplishment" -Jim Rohn.

This is exactly what I mean. When we don't have goals in life we go with the wind, East, West, North, South, any which way. We can so easily be swept away by daily distractions.

Self-discipline is the ultimate tool for achieving dreams and goals. Sometimes we have goals to achieve in life, often we fail because of a lack of self-discipline. Or to quote Jesse Owens; "We all have dreams, but in order to make dreams come into reality, it takes an awful lot of determination, dedication, self-discipline and effort". This is a very pointed kind of wisdom.

Communication in General

Effective communication is one of the important skills requires to perform well in everyday life especially in both social and profession. When you apply for a job both verbal communication as well as written communication clearly have the same status as formal qualifications and work experience. However, those skills can never advance your career without being guarded by discipline. This make me to conclude that discipline is like water in our life. If we are not disciplined, we make silly things that cost lives. For example, you can destroy a friendship/relationship with yourself if you don't have skill of how to communicate a necessary message even if it is an excellent message to convey; therefore, discipline especially self-discipline makes difference. Developing good communication skills requires discipline. Communication skills are important in all aspects of our lives, at home, at school and university, at work and whole society.

Communication at Home

"Charity begins at home" - your home is where discipline begins. There is nothing like home, in the traditional family, literally the foundation of all discipline is where you are raised and nurtured. It starts with mom, follows by dad, siblings and the rest of the extended family members, according to the way of traditional societies. Plant roots shoot from the seedling before reaching air & sun out on surface. Our community, our society and the whole world can learn from this model. Children are the roots of the family who grow strong from the family plant. Many of our (South Sudanese) kids in diaspora lost that fundamental foundation. They become generation of "don't talk to me, who are you, go away and so on?" they considered themselves more knowledgeable than their parents because they speak better English than their parents if any even though they don't properly write. They have lost respect for their parents and this can lead to lack of discipline especially at home, at school and in public space. There are some young people though who value their family and their culture like Chua A, who said "I see my upbringing as a great success story. By disciplining me, my parents inculcated self-discipline, by restricting my choices as a child, they gave me so many choices in my life as an adult. Because of what they did then, I get to do the work I love now.". Guiding our children to place of success is a better way of applying self-discipline than physical punishment. Self-discipline is in some ways an expensive kind of choice for your future, but worth taking. It is like saving money for the future, it helps in the long term but hurts in the short term. The home discipline is transferred from home to a workplace that is why it is in the family interest to build their children well in the way it suits the family unit description and the goal of discipline. Our children bear our names wherever they go, and therefore they reflect family character when it comes precipitation. One of our respected elder once said to his son, "it doesn't matter how badly you dislike me, but one thing will never change; you will never get rid of my name against your name. No one else will accept you to be his son". We are ambassadors of our parents, families and communities everywhere we go; therefore, we must understand our family values and teaching so that we realise the benefits. We would never represent our family values when we lack self-discipline. Family values are definitive and distinctive to your family and community we come from. If your family choses to act contrary to the rules of law, that shows their family values in action, and it is what children learn.

Communication and Education

Education has been extremely important in my life as it is with many and in the lives of my community in Australia. Ideally education builds on the strong foundations of discipline, loyalty and other important values established within the family. No matter how educated you might be you still need better communication guarded by discipline to be able to harvest fruits of your career.

Calvin Coolidge said "Knowledge comes, but wisdom lingers. It may not be difficult to store up in the mind a vast quantity of facts within a comparatively short time, but the ability to form judgements requires severe discipline of hard work and tempering heat of experience and maturity."

Communication at Work

"Without hard work and discipline, it is difficult to be a top professional" - Jahangir Khan. "Seek freedom and become captive of your desires. Seek discipline and find your liberty" -Frank Herbert.

We work in an environment where employees are safe in number of ways. There are rules about respectful and inclusive behaviour and there are informal cultures of how workplaces operate. It is good to be skilled and knowledgeable in both the formal and the informal aspects of work.

The workplace is where you meet many great people, but the question needs to be asked is how you get to meet them. No matter how hard we work, without self-discipline and good communication we will never reach that goal of meeting great people and reach understanding of staff in the organization. The profile and respect in which your organization is held will enhance your chances to be sent to conferences and gala dinners and this is where we meet other great people from corporations and governments and learn how to communicate with and influence all types of people.

Communication at Public Space

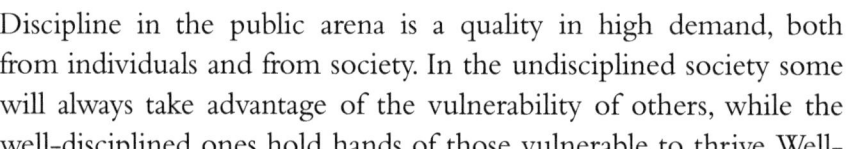

Discipline in the public arena is a quality in high demand, both from individuals and from society. In the undisciplined society some will always take advantage of the vulnerability of others, while the well-disciplined ones hold hands of those vulnerable to thrive. Well-disciplined can easily be identified even in the way they talk and walk.

Public discipline is a composition of some elements such as conformity, social norms, self-esteem, obedience, conscience, influence, fear of self-destruction, selflessness, altruism, self-respect, compliance, etc.; if you were to arm yourself with these characteristics, you would align yourself with public discipline.

You may ask where we get these characters. The answer is very simple and straightforward. It all begins in the home and from a very young age.

"Discipline is the bridge between goals and accomplishment" - Rohn, J.

"Let's not be afraid to speak the common sense ... truth: you can't have high standards without good discipline" - Hague, W.

Having been involved in a number of institutions and having believed on testing everything, makes me aware of numbers of aspects from those different fields/areas, such as the understanding of discipline as applicable both in the Military and in the Church. I am proud of myself; I am a church leader; a community leader and I have been an army officer. These experiences made me aware of many behaviours from many sectors of public order and faith. The only thing I have not been into is a celebrity! So, this does not allow me to talk more about discipline in the world of celebrities. However, discipline is discipline across all walks of life I guess, businesspeople have a particular discipline that makes them successful. Hardworking, never giving up and never giving away too much. Is that principle not wonderful and focus? These principles lead us to the very base of discipline. We do discipline ourselves because we love ourselves, we respect ourselves and have to be tolerance to earn tittles.

Tolerance, Self-Respect, and Self-Love

Discipline is a science, it need to be possessed by everyone for better society. Tolerance is more of an art - it allows you to love the good and the bad in yourself.

John Weir. "Love myself, I do. Not everything, but I love the good as well as the bad. I love my crazy lifestyle, and I love my hard discipline. I love freedom of speech and the way my eyes get dark when I'm tired. I love that I have learned to trust people with my heart, even if it will get broken. I am proud of everything that I am and will become."

Self-discipline combined with tolerance and self-love allows me to dare to dream. Even dreaming has rules and discipline according to John Maxell. You set a bar to meet. Rule one: you must embrace risk, as necessary. Rule two: rely on it when initiating and, Rule Three: create momentum to take an action. Self-discipline is a talent which gives you the power of self-confidence and ultimately success.

Successful people, sometimes fail, but persevere till they taste success. Persistence is another form of discipline. When I was in high school in Ethiopia in the early 1990s, I heard a story of an Ethiopian guy who used to be a tail of his class almost throughout his primary and secondary education. luckily, he later migrated to USA with his family and from there he went to a college where he studies till, he acquired his Ph. D in science and became a respected scientist among his peers.

"If you set goals for yourself, and you are like a lot of other people, you probably realise, it is not that your goals are physically impossible that's keeping you from achieving them; it is that you lack the self-discipline to stick to them." - Goldstein, D.

Body Language and Communication

I am taking a detour now to the complicated area of non-verbal communication which is at least as powerful as the power of the pen and forms a large part of face-to-face verbal communication. For example, the bowing or head-down gesture without looking the subject in the eye is a sign of loyalty in Dinka and some other African cultures. Young people cannot look adults in the eye; it is disrespectful when they do it. Any child who fails to follow this golden rule will be known among the community as a child who is lacking respect for elders. However, looking away or looking down has been misinterpreted in Anglo Celtic culture as dishonesty because of that cultures belief in eye contact as a demonstration of honesty.

Church Discipline – In Worship

Hands raised in the air and eyes closed, is a Christian discipline in the worship and adoration of God. There is no one there urging you to do this. You yourself as a believer know the need for concentration and meditation with God. This is an ethic of your faith in God. When you lift your hands in air, it is not a normal practice rather it is everyday thing to do when worshipping. It is done with focus in the full knowledge of what you want and switch off your mind to the world in meditation manner and spiritual speaking. Moses lifted his hand with staff at Rephidim in fight against Amalekites (Ex. 17: 8 – 15) exactly explains that kind of domain. Lift your hands and heart to the throne of the Highest. In church lifting your arms is lamentation, submissiveness and placing of a request to Most High Power. This is a Church or divine discipline.

Principle of Discipline in the Military

When I was a child, we used to be told that soldiers' photos are taken upside down as a symbol of readiness to die and that death is a possibility at any moment.

Arms behind the back is unique to the military; a code of readiness, loyalty, and submission to order from a superior. I was taught the practice of attention and management of my arms and hands. Arms straight at your side for attention and arms behind the back for standing at ease or rest ('tiba, saba') – such was the military significance of arm control and meaning.

You cannot have attention with your arm playing or swinging or you face the consequence of punishment. "Yes, Sir, I am here ready for duty Sir". It is a different kind of loyalty, but without personal gain and that is why I love it. Loyalty to your nation, to your people, to service and to yourself as a self-respecting person; being ready to defend it all with all you have.

Attention   *Ease*

Body Language

Arms crossing - the blockage/fencing brachiate one's character as Australian call it.

This is a physical attitude that I can't explain beyond what I've observed and felt while observing it. It may; however, convey different messages when talking about body language. It makes me feel comfortable and attentive while standing and listening to people talking even though I'm not part of the conversation and like to listen. However, it may somehow not conform with principle of discipline in most profession fields. It shows seriousness on the one hand and attention on the other. It could also represent a challenge directed at you by a person whom you believe not to be of your social class. The crossed arm stance can be used anywhere, but not with lion leadership bosses, however.

For my part I feel comfortable when I am standing with my arms crossing below my chest. I'm unsure how others think about it and I see many people doing it the way I do.

This is where differences may arise with different cultures. In Karen culture practices and most ethnic groups from Burma arm crossing below the chest shows respect to elders, to teachers and to persons in authority while listening.

In Australian culture, arm crossing is a brachiate or fencing off from others and for this reason this stance is sometimes seen as unacceptable. It is like looking at a person in the eye in Australian culture which is totally different in several cultures, like African cultures and Asian cultures. Brachiating is nothing offensive in my culture unless it is indicated by shoulders some indifference. Many things mean different things in different cultures though world is now global village.

Fighting external negative forces which target those with determination is not an easy battle. It is a fight that couldn't be won easily by many. It is like hyena crossing river of blood and meat without taking one piece of meat or taste of blood. The reward we collect after we crossed that swarm is countless. You can be a famous sport person, famous politician, well known scientist, renounce doctor/gynecologist, celebrity, legendary, etc. people do not even know hardship you went through, but you. This brings me to my military training experience in a hostile environment where everything was int its scarcity. In battle many external people celebrate our achievements in battlefield. In our end, it was like a deaden kind of campaign. People were not aware of how hard it was on us. No good food or no food at all for several days, no medicine or shelter when rain comes. Many necessities were missing, but there were more celebrations externally.

My Second Escape in the Place I call Home (South Sudan)

I became one of the escapees from Bor, on the 18th of December 2013, from a crisis that I had no power to alter or avert. I want to tell my story to enlighten our community in Australia about what had happened in South Sudan, especially concerning the humanitarian crisis of December 2013/January 2014.

I was in Bor, South Sudan when war broke out in December 2013 in South Sudan after only two years of its independence from the Sudan.

This is what happened to me and my family in December 2013. I call it my second escape from Bor (the place I call home), I escaped the 1983 war from the same place.

I left Australia with my son Kuol, my cousin Peter Jongroor and my nephew Chol Jongroor on the 2nd of December 2013 for South Sudan. My sister Mary (Aluel) had left Australia two days ahead of us, on the 30th of November, with her three sons and step-son. We had no inkling that something dangerous lay ahead on that momentous visit to our mum and brothers. The other person we travelled on separate dates was our last-born Machar Kuol.

Our travel to South Sudan was mainly to do with family affairs. My son Kuol had not previously met any of my family members who are in South Sudan, including his grandmother, his two uncles (my brothers), aunties and cousins, nephews, nieces and extended family members. I have nine uncles (my dad's maternal brothers); and in average each have at less 15 children. This makes my family a large family in our community. It is very important for us to take our children to the country we call home especially those who were not born there to meet our extended families.

Four of us (Peter, Chol, Kuol and I) arrived in Juba, the capital of South Sudan, on the 3$^{rd.}$ of December 2013. We devoted our first two weeks there to celebrate Peter's marriage before we proceeded to Bor to join up with my brothers, cousins, sisters, and other nephews. Then three of us (Chol, Kuol and I) plus my brother Akau who joined us in Juba, left for Bor-town on 15th December in the morning. At 9pm fighting broke out in Juba, which is 200km away from Bor.

What happened in Juba on Dec 15th 2013 was something that had been anticipated and I believe many people who watched or listened to the President's speech on the 14th in the SPLM conference would definitely agree with my view plus other rumours that were out there. Those rumours were strengthened by the meeting held on 6th Dec 2013 by other SPLM leaders (Dr. Riek, Dr Majak, Deng Alor, Pagan Amum, Rebecca Nyandeng plus more). President Salva Kiir was very antagonistic towards one person in particular, Dr Riek Machar, the

Vice President, at one time considered a traitor who had also been responsible for oil drilling which benefited the Arab north regime during the 1990s split of SPLA/M. I was so concerned, then I asked my cousins, who has just happened to be placed in reserve list, Lt General Gabriel Ayuen. My question to him was why our President attacked his deputy openly like that! Because at the time my heart started to tremble about the future of that country for the fact that I knew Riek's tribal behaviour, I knew how Kiir's community thinks too. I told myself that something bad would happen. It was not long before many voices in the ruling party were not pleased with the direction in which the party was channelling its affairs. I told them (my cousins) that, had it been up to me, I would have not chosen to use the language or tone that the President was now using. The president language is too provocative.

That speech was on Saturday at the opening of the National Liberation Council (NLC) conference, on the 14th of December in Juba. My fear was that either Riek would rebel against the government led by President Salva, or Salva would confront Riek on the pretext that he intended to betray the South Sudanese people again, as he put it in his speech, that he would never allow 1991 history to repeat itself and he has never betrayed his people. I am not quite sure of what really happened on that day (the 15th) or how it happened, but I am pretty sure one of my fears was realised.

Back to what happened in Bor-town on the 18th, it was the same destabilising affair as occurred in Juba. After the so-called failed coup attempt on the 15th in Juba surfaced, the killing of the Nuer ethnic population in Juba was rumoured to have occurred. Bor, the town which was predominantly populated by ethnic Nuer in term of army was overrun by Division 8 led by the notorious former Arab militia leader, Major General Peter Gadet who hails from Unity State (Nuer). In the course of his career, he had changed sides sometimes (18 times) between the Sudanese People's Liberation Army/ Movement (SPLA/M) and Khartoum regime (Arab North) during the liberation struggle (1983 -2011). The easy defeat of Bor by this group occurred because many of the Nuer militia, who had been changing side were observed to be in the South Sudan army after the 2005 peace agreement between the SPLM (South) and National Congress Party (NCP, Khartoum) and some after independence in 2011 were stationed there which was completely wrong. The downside of this is that the majority of them were based in Bor and all over Jonglei state, including part of Upper Nile and Juba itself. Those militiamen lack discipline and lack an understanding of the role of the army and national duty, but loyal to their tribe. They only observe their tribal alliance. According to information I got, the Tiger unit (presidential guard) was mainly composed of Paulino Matip militia (Nuer). In the unit there were 42 generals and among these generals only two are from different tribes while 40 are from Nuer community.

Maj. Gen. Peter Gadet was the first to express his discontent with the government, after being accused himself of massive human rights abuses committed under his command against Murle civilians in Jonglei state during an operation against David Yau Yau rebel earlier in 2013. Gadet was called to report to the military headquarter in Bilpham, Juba, but refused and barricaded himself in his own headquarters at Panpandiar, Bor (Division 8 headquarters). After several consultations and assurances that he was not going to be arrested, he went to Juba. At headquarters I do not know what happened. He was then ordered to remain in Bor, Division 8 headquarter. One of his conditions he put to the leadership was that he was not to remain in Bor unless 5 of his generals who happen to be from Bor were removed from Division 8 which he commands. That condition was considered by the President and by the head of the military (Central Command). That was when my cousin Brig. General Abraham Jongroor, Maj. General Ajak Yen and Major General Tour Alier were deployed to join him (Abraham and Ajak both got killed, though they were not killed on the same day). Maj. Gen. Ajak was the first casualty of 18th Dec. killed by Peter himself in a pretended meeting.

The reason why I knew most of Gadet's problems, many people may question credibility of my story. On 5/12/13 I had a meeting with one of 5 Generals that Gadet didn't want in Division 8, I asked him the reason behind their transfer from the Division 8. He told me frankly and I quote "If Gadet is going to live in peace, then we have no problem..., my personal concern is that Gadet is not going to stay there peacefully and I'm afraid he will leave Bor peacefully". He further added "I think the government is transferring us just to please Gadet which I believe won't work". What this General (I don't want to mention his name) told me was later confirmed by General Abraham before he headed to Bor with General Ajak on 6/12/13.

On the 16th the fighting intensified in Juba between government forces and rebels. Bor residents felt the heat by the very fact that the whole army in Jonglei state was dominated by one tribe (Nuer) and activities they were doing were not in favour of everybody else, but their own; however, there was nothing those in civilian government nor Bor residents could possibly do to control the situation. There was also no way for civilians to leave Bor for capital because Juba is the only way out of Bor in case of safety. The military barracks of Malual Chaat, Panpandiar and Pariak lie on the route to Juba, and two of those barracks were controlled by the rebel (Gadet forces). About 4pm on the afternoon of the 16th about 200 metres away from where I was living one person was shot dead and another one was wounded by Nuer gangs (the police); they were on their motor bike, and both were from Bor county.

The situation reached some boiling point in the morning of the 17th in Bor town: two brothers who had decided to stay behind to protect their properties in the block (4) where the shooting had occurred on the afternoon of the 16th were found dead. By that time, all adjacent blocks had been deserted by people who did not hail from the Nuer community. Both young men were killed in execution style, their throats were cut with knives while their heads were hacked with a machete.

This killing happened after the authorities and the people of the Bor community had tried everything they could to avert this foreseeable human catastrophe. All their efforts in the end achieved no tangible result. They were not able to save lives nor calm down the situation.

The killing terrified the whole of the town's population. People began leaving the town for the bush in panic from 2pm on the 17th. The Nuer population headed to the south of the town where the barracks and the UNMIS were and the Jieng (Dinka) headed northward to hide in the bush. Some people, including myself and my family, chose to ignore the panic and stay put. As darkness unfolded, many houses were looted. The exodus continued throughout the night before the actual military mutiny occurred in both the military barracks of Panpandiar and Malual Chaat. Exactly at 12am and 2am respectively on the 18th both barracks were in full control of rebellion. General Ajak Yen was the casualty of 12am in hand of Gadet. He was lured for a meeting and short on head in execution style.

When shooting started at Panpandiar at 12am on the 18th, many of my relatives in Juba (armed force members) called me and urged me to leave the area immediately with anybody of our family members who were still in the block. All of cousins who were calling from Juba were monitoring Bor's situation very closely for the fact that Maj Gen Gadet was well known to be on the edge of rebellion. General Abraham was fourth in command of Division 8, but he was at his recent in Juba, he was almost got killed on 16th Dec. 2013. His resident was between Mangateen and Bilpham (Military headquarter) and Captain Madul was one of the officers in the Panyier military training centre in Bor. It was a sleepless night I tell you. I came out to observe the aerial firefight above me in the sky. While I was still outside monitoring the situation, fighting erupted at the Malual Chaat barracks, the nearest barrack. I could even feel the vibration under my feet from the barrage of heavy artillery shells. The time was 2am.

As the situation continued deteriorating, everyone except my mother agreed to leave. She became ill from the stress of the unexpected situation. Her daughter, Mary (Aluel) with four children and the three of us (my son, my younger brother and I) had just arrived from Australia. Two brothers with their families came too from a refugee camp in Uganda and a cattle camp in Western Equatoria to meet us. It was a good family reunion. I had not seen some of my family members for over 30 years, while my brother had not seen our mum for 26 years (1987 – 2013), let alone the rest of our family members. My brother Machar had spent only 4 days in town, and my son, nephew and I had just been in the town for 3 days restlessly trying to finalise number of outstanding family issues.

It was a chaotic scene from 2 am until 11am in all four directions (West to the river Nile, north to Athooch, east to Juorkoch & Pale and south to Juorhol) people were so panicking. The exodus of animals (cows, goats, and sheep) and humans from the town was unprecedented, the most chaotic departure I have ever seen. The only situation I could possibly compare with-it would-be May 1983 when we were leaving Bor & May 1991 when we were fleeing Ethiopia.

The thought that invaded my mind was where would they go after this! It was an incomprehensible situation to me and those who were with me. Children were running about without parents, and there was no available food or water. Your only thought was to grab & hold of a few personal belongings on your way out of the house. Many people were totally lost, especially those who had not been in Bor since the 1980s. Foreign nationals were particularly confused (Ethiopians, Kenyans, Ugandans, Somalis, etc.).

At around 6:30 am (18/12/13) before my phone run out of power, Rachel my wife rang from Australia after several failed attempts to get in touch with us. She was in tears and I told her that we are all together except my sister Mary, but we were in communication with her. Mary was in a bad location and it worried us a lot; she was very close to the Malual Chaat military barracks outside town with one younger son and daughter while her other three sons were on the far side of the Malual Chaat military barracks. We called her to come to us so that we could plan an escape route together. Unfortunately, she was holding all passports of the other kids. Then she decided to send to us the young son (Kuol) who happened to be with her at the time because it was still safe for him (as a young child) to come to where we were.

In my talk with Rachel what came to my mind was how we could do to help those hopeless people, so I told her to inform NGOs especially the Red Cross whether in Juba or in Australia to at least let them know about the exodus of the population, because I was out of ideas. Then, think of how they could supply them with water and food for the day. Thanks to Rachel, she tried many channels which I couldn't even think of. It was about 2pm Australia Eastern standard time (6am East Africa time). Rachel did a fantastic job for us; she registered us with the Department of Foreign Affairs and Trade (DAFT) Australia.

At 9am my older brother decided to call for a boat from Guolyar on the other side of River Nile, the West bank; this later became the main route to escape the killing. People from Guolyar responded positively and sent a boat for us and that was the time Abraham Majak and his brother Chol joined us because they were in communication with Machar (my younger brother). The boat cost us dearly and, according to those who came after us, we had a better deal than those who followed. At about 11:45am we boarded the boat and headed for Guolyar, which took us about 3 hours to get to the far shore of the river. On that day, many boats were to follow. Guolyar on that very day established itself as an internal displaced persons' camp (IDPs camp) for the people of Bor-town.

At Guolyar camp there was no building to accommodate Internal Displaced Persons (IDPs), not even newly born babies (meaning those born between the 15th and 20th of December). People had to fight to get a tree for their families to shelter them from the heat of the blistering sun (the temperature was in between $30°$ and $45°$). You can imagine a population of between 70,000 or 100,000 gathering in an area lacking large trees. Too, no primary humanitarian basic needs available whatsoever.

Escaping the fighting was one of the dangers, but hunger and disease were the other inescapable threats for the people of Bor in Guolyar. Many children reportedly died within two weeks of arriving in the camp, according to a report from former Bor county commissioner

Hon. Maker Lual that diarrhoea struck the camp, he wrote, at least 20 children died in that period.

Our escape route was not a safe one at all. We were gambling with our lives because there was no other choice available but to seek a way out. My sadness particularly was that my son and two nephews had been in South Sudan less than a month, this human tragic and all-encompassing memories that they would have of South Sudan will never go away.

Humanitarian Appeal

All of us who love the people of South Sudan did whatever we could to support those who lost everything. My wife Rachel and I reached out to many organisations including rotary clubs, National Australia Bank where she works and church agencies like Anglican Overseas Aid & Anglican Diocese of Melbourne in Australia to support our campaign of generating support to displaced persons. I have to use my story of escape from that conflict on 18/12/2013 in Bor, with my son, nephews, brothers and friends to help Anglican Overseas Aid and Anglican Communion Worldwide to raise $2m urgently needed in areas of Warrap State, Lake State and Upper Nile State to people who were in the greatest need of support. The way we left people in at most parts of South Sudan particularly Guolyar was not comprehensible in term of food, shelters and health. Government was not in a position of providing anything to anyone at any stage, particularly in first few months of the conflict. Government wasn't coping with its own immediate response, the military operation. Therefore, I must try all ways to ignite my network which I have to start with my wife (where she works, National Australian Bank), Anglican Overseas Aid (AOA) where I was doing my internship then connect with all other spiritual leaders of our Church, Revd. Peter Jongroor, David Lual, Revd. Daniel Amol & Revd. Daniel Ateny. Then we started to lodge an appeal with imagination to ourselves in the same dire situation in which we found ourselves in at that time. This appeal led to series of meetings and consultations with Anglican Communion and Acts Alliance all over the world and use my story as a starting point. Us on boat crossing River Nile to Gualyar to show how serious the situation was.

Abraham (centre) with his brother and boat driver as they fled accross the Nile to safety in Dec 2013.

My name is Abraham Jongroor from Melbourne. In 2013 I escaped violence in my homeland, South Sudan – for the second time. I had taken my 10-year-old son Kuol to South Sudan for the very first time to meet my large extended family, and particularly his grandmother.

We arrived in my hometown of Bor on December 15 – the very day that Government factions started fighting in the capital, Juba, 151km/94 miles to the south of Bor. Early in the morning of December 18 relatives called, urging us to leave immediately. We quickly grabbed everything we could carry and fled the town with thousands of others as army units started their rebellion, going on a rampage of violence and destruction.

My uncle's wife was shot dead after she returned to Bor to feed the elderly who had been unable to come with us.

To escape, we had to catch boats across the Nile, pay a driver for a full day trip to another region and then catch a small plane to the capital Juba on second day. From here we were evacuated by British Royal Airforce (RAF) Hercules to Uganda, before finally getting on flights back to Melbourne. In all, our escape took 10 stressful days back to Australia.

Our escape route was not a safe one. We were gambling with our lives but there was no other choice. It was a terrible ordeal, but as Australian citizens, my son and I can return to the safety of our wonderful country. We left behind many others who cannot escape. The United Nations says that more than half a million people have been forced from their homes, with most of them remaining inside South Sudan and in need of urgent assistance. Many of these people are family and friends of Australia's South Sudanese community, who were waiting anxiously to find out if they are alive or dead.

Back in Australia, it was a rare moment when refugees from a national crisis can advise an Australian agency on the next crisis. But that is what has happened with the new South Sudanese civil war between Dinka and Nuer tribes.

Four South Sudanese who are elders in Anglican parishes in Melbourne today became advisers to Anglican Overseas Aid in how to respond to the crisis. They are the Rev. Daniel Kuol Amol of Dandenong, Abraham Jongroor, community development worker of Melton, the Rev. Daniel Bol Nyieth of North Melbourne, and David Lual Mabior of Ringwood.

Each of these elders and many others in Melbourne have lost relatives in the current armed conflict, which has focused on the town of Bor near the White Nile River, where most refugees in Australia have come from.

Ten of them were visiting family for Christmas when the trouble broke out. "It is not tribal, it is political," said David Mabior. And

Daniel Kuol Amol said: "If the two leaders – the President and Vice President – can't meet around the table, we write to them and say, 'this must stop'."

Anglican Overseas Aid international program manager Janice Lucas has been in urgent touch during the past week with ACT Alliance, and other international interchurch networks about the best way to provide emergency relief around the towns of Bor and Guolyar, with a view to shaping an appeal to Australian churches to donate to a special emergency appeal. This network has the support of the Archbishop of Juba and the Archbishop of Canterbury.

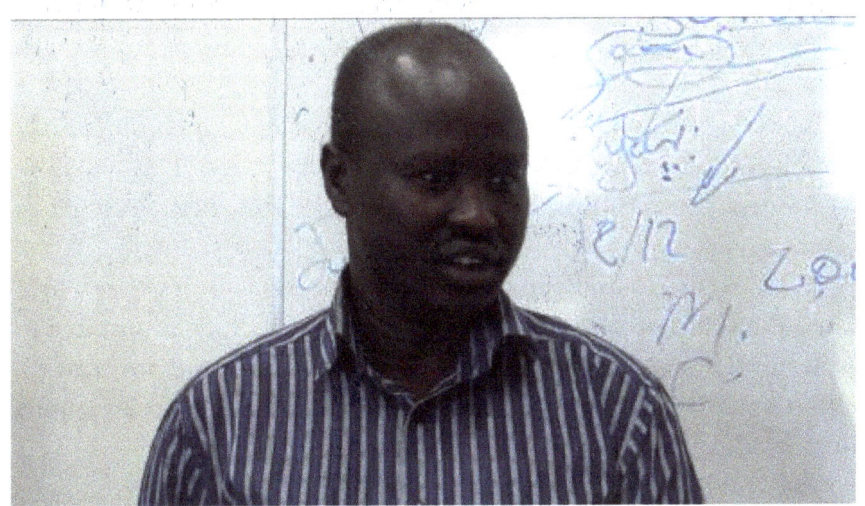

Abraham Jongroor

Today community worker Abraham Jongroor briefed AOA on what has been happening in South Sudan. He was in Bor himself visiting his family for Christmas and introducing his ten-year-old son to them, when armed conflict broke out in his neighbourhood. His relatives escorted him to safety, and he finally got to Kampala where he caught a plane back to Melbourne.

Abraham Jongroor explained how 70,000 people in Bor fled across the White Nile River to Guolyar, where they became isolated, without food, medicine, or shelter. Unconfirmed reports indicate as many as 20,000 died, and many others were stricken by cholera living in the open without shelter. As well, families are raising finance to enable or two of their family to cross into Uganda and claim refugee status. For many, their homes and villages have been completely destroyed, and there is nothing to go home to.

David Mabior said: "This has been mind-breaking for us, it was such a shock. It was Christmas time, but people were collapsing. In the Sudanese churches here in Melbourne, we started praying about this, and praying with Pentecostal and other churches. In this network there are prayers every Friday for four hours from 10am.

"People are getting bad news from Facebook and emails, and our elders said to them: We are donors, not just receivers of aid. We can contribute."

In a congregation of 400 in Clayton Anglican Church on January 1, they collected $3,000 in cash as a first contribution. This will now be the first donation towards an appeal to be launched by Anglican Overseas Aid.

AOA executive director Bob Mitchell, at the end of the briefing, asked the four Sudanese to be on an ongoing advisory committee to assist AOA in making decisions about an appeal and its consequences. David Mabior said: "It's now a disaster everywhere, even in the capital Juba. It's short term but it will also be long term."

The Sudanese group acknowledged the contributions of the Australian Government so far – an initial grant and a loan of two aircraft to assist evacuations. They next look to the Church to make its response. David Mabior added: "Pray especially for children, who die and don't even know what has happened to them. And we pray for the suffering to cease."

In closing the briefing, the Rev. Daniel Nyieth prayed for peace to come in this conflict, which had broken out unexpectedly only two years after South Sudan became an independent nation following 20 years of war with north Sudan.

Janice Lucas with Abraham Jongroor

Alan Nichols

Instate of them being concern and phrase God for how they came back to safe and sound with kids and everybody else who was with us to Australia. Our safety and projects we embarked on was an important one and touches everyone who knows us and those who like humanity works. Most were even concern of how I could get those kids to safety.

Thank you very much Bob for your concern. My son and I are Ok, we are now in Kampala. However, situation is still extremely difficult to those who are left behind. My sister with her two sons is still in Bor area, the worse hit area.

The violence started on 17/12/13 in Bortown where we were living just 500 metres away from my mum's house. We were sleeping then on 18/12/13 the violence escalated to extreme from 12am. At 2am my cousins who were military personals, but base in Juba 200Km away from Bor rang us and order us to immediately leave Bortown by any mean. We didn't waste time, immediately started our journey by foot then on boat at 11am to other side of River Nile which took us at least three hours. Then on 19/12/13 we hired a car to take us to Rumbek the Capital of lake state where we believe we may board a plane that will take us to Juba where we may get evacuation flight. That was another journey of whole day (9am - 6:30pm). On 20/12/13 we managed to board a commercial flight from Rumbek to Juba. At our arrival we got British Royal military air force Hercules evacuating British, New Zealanders and Australian nationals, at that point we didn't waste much time, so we have to register with them, as soon as we finish registration, we boarded the plane which took us to Kampala, Uganda on the same day (20/12/13). Now we are in Kampala and will leave Kampala for Melbourne on 25/12/13. In the middle of an appeal there was no time to be wasted.

Thursday 20 March 2014
Dear David Lual Mabior and members of the South Sudanese Anglican churches,

Greetings to you all. I am writing to update you on the South Sudan Emergency Appeal. We are able to report on funding raised so far, although do not yet have written reports back from ACT Alliance partners. We can report what had been raised by end of February has been sent to partner agencies working in South Sudan and more is accumulating. Based on telephone meetings and communications from the Anglican Alliance, we can also report that progress is being made on the ground and this is starting to make a difference.

Background

Anglican Overseas Aid was approached by the South Sudanese Anglican community in Melbourne to start an appeal and work alongside parishes to raise an awareness of the conflict and need for relief and peace building in South Sudan. Anglican Overseas Aid, in

Displaced women disembark from a boat that has brought them back home to Bor, a city in South Sudan's Jonglei State that was been the scene of fierce fighting in 2013 between the country's military and anti-government rebels. After fighting broke out in mid-December 2013, control of the town changed hands four times in a few weeks. ACT Alliance members were among the first humanitarian agencies to enter the city in January 2014, and are providing services to thousands of people who are cautiously returning home to the troubled city. These women have crossed the While Nile River from Awerial, where they took refuge. Photo: ACT Alliance/Paul Jeffrey

communication with a steering group of South Sudanese church leaders, set up an appeal in January 2014 to raise awareness and funds for relief support in South Sudan.

Appeal Funds Channel

In the case of the recent conflict in South Sudan, the ACT Alliance raised US$9,176,186 appeal through an appeal. Partner agencies included: Norwegian Church Aid (NCA), World Renew, Dan Church Aid (DCA), Finn church Aid (FCA), ICCO and KIA, Christian Aid, and Lutheran World Federation (LWF).

Initial plans were for the partner agencies to work in at least seven of South Sudan's 10 states, focusing on Jonglei, Unity, Upper Nile and Central Equatoria. Response activities include food, non-food items (NFIs), WASH (water, sanitation and hygiene), education, child protection, health, shelter, psycho-social support, early recovery and reintegration, advocacy, and coordination.

A decision was made for initial AOA funds to go to Norwegian Church Aid, as their plan was explicitly to work through existing church structures, in particular one being the Episcopal Church of Sudan and South Sudan, and through SUDRA (their Sudanese Development and Relief Agency). At the same time, other Anglican partners such as ABM and ERD (US) provided direct support to SUDRA through their existing partnerships, helping to support communications and recruitment and capacity of new staff. There are also specific agreements from other agencies such as Christian Aid and Tearfund UK that are supporting SUDRA with generators and funding for their food appeal. NCA and LWF are now also supporting IDPs, those displaced in the bush and returnees in Bor. See link below for latest report (March 17) on ACT progress in Bor: http://www.actalliance.org/stories/hope-in-the-ashes-of-bor.

South Sudanese Progress

So far, $7005 has been raised from the church and public. Anglican Overseas Aid has increased this by $5366, and a total of $10,000 AUD has so far been sent in the first tranche overseas. The $10,000 has been sent through the ACT Alliance as specifically nominated for the NCA plan. The recent fortnightly report back from SUDRA is that NCA is sending a number of containers from Mombasa with non-food items through to them to support the current ECSSS SUDRA appeal (with support from existing partners, SUDRA has put together about $200,000 for food funding, which is being shipped north).

As well as the work that the ACT Alliance members do in advocacy and communications, the Anglican Alliance is also engaging in advocacy and supporting messages and important information from South Sudan to be shared across the world. At the same time the Alliance is directly encouraging ECSSS/SUDRA with visits and regular communications and enabling partners to collaborate better and more effectively through facilitating networking and joint dialogue.

AOA has successfully managed to raise awareness of the appeal through a number of channels.

The main story that we have used is about the experience of Abraham Jongroor, who was in Bor with his son when the fighting started and had a 10-day journey to evacuate and return to Melbourne.

Based on this story, we have managed to get information about the appeal out broadly, including:
- On the website of the Bible Society of Australia
- In The Melbourne Anglican and shared on their social media channels.
- Globally through the Anglican News Service website based in Canterbury, England.
- Globally through Anglican Alliance online platforms.
- Globally through the ACT Alliance.
- There is also ongoing interest in the story from The Age newspaper, who have asked to be kept informed of developments.

We have put information about the appeal:
- On our website,
- Social media accounts such as Facebook and Twitter.
- We sent out eNews updates to all supporters.
- An article in our new newsletter, distributed to all supporters and beyond.

The South Sudanese church leaders steering group that is meeting with AOA is planning to run a service at St Paul's Cathedral at a relevant time, to bring together praying and concerned Christian supporters and to raise awareness further.

ACT Alliance have recently sent communications staff in and have started sharing quality images and stories, that we will be able to use (see front page).

Abraham and Rachel are planning for a fundraising breakfast at NAB headquarters on May 14. We are exploring who will be able to speak from the Church and AOA and NAB are supportive and will be promoting the session.

The South Sudanese churches continue to meet regularly to pray and share about how best to respond and are happy to share their experience and knowledge with other Anglican parishes as required.

AOA continues to share information about the appeal and current situation through its online communications, with information received from the churches and the fortnightly telecom with SUDRA and the Anglican Alliance.

Follow Up

It will be helpful to receive more information and stories and photos from SUDRA and ACT and this will help our appeals.

Any reports back from the ACT partners or the SUDRA team will be shared with the steering group when they are received.

We will need to consider carefully how best to continue to raise awareness and support in the community.

As mentioned before, a plan to promote an Anglican service is being developed.

A fundraising event is planned with the NAB.

When the next substantial amount is raised, we need to meet to discuss how to transfer this, either through ACT and NCA again, or if possible, more directly to the Jonglei area directly through ECSSS/SUDRA via existing partners such as ERD.

We would suggest meeting again in April, unless the situation changes beforehand.

As this appeal was going on, my wife and I never stop there, beside we decided to let her take time off work and visit displaced people of Jonglei in Lake State and refugees in number of refugee camps in Uganda. With her visit we asked our Rotary club if they could be able to provide us with any lighter equipment that Rachel Riak could carry. As a result, they provided us with two water purification systems known as Aquaboxes, they could be used in children centres. It was an idea came to mind reading a report from Bor commissioner Hon.

Maker Lual Kuol. The report indicated that in cause of two weeks, they lost more than 20 children to diarrhea suspected to be cholera due to exposure to a non-merciful circumstance. What happen when you are self-centred is never mind of feeling of others due to foreseen danger. This is exactly what Mr. Kuol described in below article he wrote exactly on subject matter.

Indiscipline Nature

There is little impossibility that the nature of a mature person can be changed. The evil abiding in individual's nature can sometimes be tamed though it is very challenging. Some degree of evil can be tamed through discipline (punishment) and some can end up in life imprisonment or state sanctioned execution or heat successful individuals. This is a kind of bad jealousy. Jealousy is divided into two parts, bad one and good one. Most people consider jealousy as bad character, but I see it in two dimensions. The bad one is when you dislike success of others and good one is the one that you create a competition. You don't like to be looked down upon; therefore, you have to be creative and create your own success with leverage of using your friends' success as a platform. I love that kind of jealousy, I wish most people would have it, especially bad jealous ones. I call it fair and healthy competition.

Moses, the Israelite boy was a wild and hot-tempered boy. According to the Bible, he was chosen to lead the Israelites out of Egypt because of his hardline approach to things, in other words, his drive and determination. Therefore, there is the opportunity for every character to do good things for community and humanity in general. It may seem contradictory in the next paragraph, but this is the reality, as we see things through different lenses.

Some people lacking discipline can be left lingering about in the community without proper management but with management support and self-discipline or can assume a leadership role. These are the kinds of people who stir problems/issues in communities.

In 1991 when Riek Machar and Lam Akol rebelled against Dr John Garang and targeted none Cholo and Nuer members in their movement, especially Jieng was the main enemy, which even weaken their success in removing Dr John Garang from SPLA/M leadership. Some of colleagues and I decided not to participate in a meaningless war. We called it a meaningless war because Riek and Lam Akol, instead of targeting our common enemy, the Khartoum Regime, they turned their weapons against their fellow comrades in the liberation struggle.

My friends and I decided to go back to Ethiopia to pursue our education. Before we could go Communication was our very best tool. We thought, talked, shared and planned under difficult circumstances of MI (military intelligence). Everyone was under the surveillance of MI because there was no trust (even among comrades in arms) after Riek and Lam were making a lot of dramas even with food relief agencies were on their side. All food relief was flown direct to Nassir including those supposed to come to Pakook or Pochala.

As we crossed to Ethiopia after few days in the bush, we came across with 'Oyano' Soldiers, Ethiopian rebel fighters at midnight at 'Kor Deng Majok'. They managed to capture some of our comrades, and the rest of us ran and hide. After a while in hiding, we came back and surrendered. We were scared to the core because they were fought off by the SPLA in May and June of that year (1991). In the end, after a spell of interrogation, we spent some time with them and became friends and started work on how to get their stuck military truck out of the sand dune in the middle koor (creek). In the morning we asked them why they were there. They told us that their truck bogged itself in sand and they been there for few days because they are left without any option, while they said the truck was still sinking anyway. Then we offered our help, which was a surprise to them. They had been in that place for more than 3 days and they had tried everything in their powers to move the truck. Anyway, after two hours of work with our help the truck was out. They were so surprised of the technique I used to get them moving. There is no friendship without good communication. The friendship with rebel was built through better and cordial communication.

Indiscipline

Indiscipline incites unrest in number of ways anywhere any time in our society even in institution like Church, governments, and cultural settings. It does in social setup and political set up. It makes people claim what is not belong to them though they clearly know it. It makes people pretend to be the one who will bring needed change or establish "truth"! Indiscipline makes you hate others or system for unknown reason. It makes you not like to see other succeed or reach a certain peak though you know you can't even make an inch in their footstep.

A MATTER OF DISCIPLINE

Assumption and ill-conclusion on matter is an indiscipline act. Please don't assume and conclude malicious act against your sister or brother on something you are not sure of or have tangible information about. This kind of ill thinking distances us from our friends and our families. Furthermore, it limits our social interaction and progress. I experienced this in number of ways, especially among South Sudanese. In the end we all be losers. Working together in harmony makes us prosper beyond imagination whether politically, socially, or economically. In this sense I consider indiscipline as enemy of progress in sociology and order of living.

I was one time verbally attacked based on assumption by someone who consider himself as a leader and an elder. His action was based on a conspiracy and misleading information relayed to him by one of people I entrusted to represent us in a Parish committee (vestry). It was very funny when I think about it and it tempted me even to question some people's intuitions and sense of analysis. I, one times asked these very people if we could open an account with Anglican Development Fund (ADF) as future fund for church construction back home (South Sudan). It was positively agreed, but no one came back for implementation. Few months later my uncle and myself actioned it. We opened the account under church offset account so that it assists in keeping parish's loan interest low, then my wife and I agreed to direct debit our 10% into that account. The amount kept building exponentially. As such, it always appears in Parish monthly financial report. This wrong mindset individual doesn't even understand transaction in the report where does this money come from or goes. If this amount keeps increasing every month without withdrawal, then something must be investigated further before I could let my conspiracy out to mislead others. He then reported it to his brother and the earlier mentioned elder that on monthly bases Parish paid Abraham $15 + k. Who on earth could believe that? Even Archbishop of the Diocese doesn't get that much per month, but with these pathetic minds, it was taken and puffed without proper scrutiny. See how indiscipline works!

Indiscipline builds inappropriate conspiracies around us always. However, do not forget what I mentioned before that there is productive jealousy, especially competition jealousy. The form of jealousy that you don't need to be looked down by your peers. The jealousy that we need to build the same level of status or higher status of our peers.

I was one time uneasy to manage soldier but respected by like minds superior. Cowardice superiors used to hate me most because I was so disobedient soldier when it comes to order in battlefield. With brave ones, I was the one they want to go to battlefield with. It was my area of indiscipline, but for the sympathy of the movement & its people it was right to do. No matter what happened, I won't let enemy pass without telling them hey, we are here to stop you. One of these situations, was when we were at Liangary county, Jubek (central Equatoria) State in early 1988. I went for hunting for a game meat as there was no food. I was caught up in midst of sneaking in enemy convoy at the rear of our ambush line. There was nothing I could possibly do to alert my comrades, but to attack the enemy myself alone. In that case I believe, my indiscipline saved lives that day. We were under sanction of not going for hunt from commander. What do you think would had occurred on that they if I would had listened to that order of not leaving the station? However, don't be socially indiscipline.

Instead of these irresponsible individuals appreciating us of what we are doing on their behalf, they opted into damaging us (family) socially as family and went out with rumours of assassinating our characters that we have been paid lump sum of money by Church every month and we are not sharing it with them. So shameful, they didn't know that the container I took to refugee camps in Uganda in Nov 2014 was funded by my family from collecting all items from individuals and families then transport them from Melbourne to Kenya and to Uganda. Then my air ticket to Kampala − Uganda and road transport from Kampala to Kenya and back on road to Uganda refugee camps and secondary school in Western Kampala and finally flight to South Sudan. This shameful thinking started after I was asked by Church to talk about anything I been through in my life and recent journey to Africa. The thing that I should talk about in my mind was my humanitarian services journey and volunteering.

In Perspectives

This is a suffering of people uncalled for. 2013 Bor Killing: A Massacre for Federalism

By Maker Lual Kuol

Riek Macar during his visit to Nairobi between 27th and 31st May 2014 called for a Federal System of Government in South Sudan. That was his reason for orchestrating the massacre of over 2000 innocent civilians in Bor on the 17th of December 2013 as a price for his demand.

Our great fathers and uncles; Stansilous Abdalla Pyasam, Elijah Ajith Mayom, Fr. Satarnino, Joseph Oduho, Both Diu, Choor Malek, Sirisio Iro, Elia Lupe, Paramena Bul Koch and the rest of the 40 members of the Liberal Party in the 1957 Constituent Assembly called for the Federal System of Government in Sudan but did not kill South

Sudanese for it!! Instead, the Northern Arabs slapped them in the face by handing over the power to the military Regime of General Ibrahim Abud on the 17th November 1958 as a way of cuffing their mouths.

By the way who designed the current system of decentralization in South Sudan of 10 states and 79 counties? Is Riek Macar not one of the architects?

After the sad incidents of last year, December 15th 2013 and after a massive loss to thousands of lives, displacement of millions and destruction of property and infrastructure, Riek Macar, the orchestrator of the massacre of the over 2000 innocent people of Bor County, dressed up nicely in his smart attire thinking he can get applauses from the easily forgetful and forgiving South Sudanese and blindfold them with a demand for [a Federal System of Government in South Sudan] as a solution. The demand for federalism at this particular moment when people are mourning their loved ones is like congratulating the relatives of the deceased on the death of their loved ones. I thought it was time to console ourselves on the great losses and suffering faced by our people during the six months period. Who has the mind and the gut to concentrate when thousands are dead and millions roaming on their face in the jungles and bushes of South Sudan or refugee camps in the neighboring countries!!

OK, in examining the call for federalism and unfortunately some are demanding it as a matter of experiment! This means if it fails, people must kill other more South Sudanese and put up another proposal for another system of rule and we keep on experimenting and killing.

Federalism was the call of our great fathers and uncles, Elijah Ajith Mayom, Serisio Iro, Stansilaus Abdalla Pyasama, Choor Malek, Both Dieu, Parmena Bul Koch, Fr. Satarnino, Joseph Oduho, Elia Lupe and all the rest of the 40 members of South Sudanese in the second parliament in 1957 but the successive despotic regimes in Khartoum continued to throw the requests into the faces of our people and for intimidation and cuffing of mouths, Northerners ushered in many military governments into power in Khartoum. When Numiery

Regime seized power in May 1969, it worked out the regional system in Southern Sudan which in my opinion and opinion of others was equivalent to the claimed Federalism. When Southern Sudanese were moving steadily on their own besides conflicting personal interests of some South Sudanese, the North came in and abrogated the Addis Ababa Agreement and split Southern Region into three regions against the wish of South Sudanese. And because of the incessant interference of the North in the affairs of South Sudan, South Sudanese took to arms for the second time that culminated into the current independence of South Sudan.

While SPLM/A was waging the war of liberation, there were governments going on in South Sudan especially the Coordination Council for the South equivalent in powers, even if nominal, to the powers of the defunct Regional Government of Southern Sudan. Though away (I) with other thousands in the struggle, many coordination Council Governments and chairmen changed hands. And if not mistaken, James Loro, Dr. Riek Machar, Dr. Riek Gai, Lual Lual Akuei and General Gatluak Deng changed chairs on those governments. Even the inherited system of states and counties was influenced by the mentioned Chairpersons. It was not coincidence that some areas received better shares in decentralization than others. Greater Aweil, the known largest greater district in the whole of Southern Sudan in the past ended up with 5 counties and Greater Bentiu garnered 9 counties (Almost doubling Aweil) leave its equivalence like Greater Bor that walked away with only three counties; that means greater Bentiu is three times greater Bor in both population and counties!

The call of Riek Macar for federalism is that the killing of tens of thousands of people by him, displacement of millions and destruction of property could not be substantiated by him. Why was federalism raised at this particular moment and was not raised during the 8 years period when Riek Machar was the vice president of the republic? Does Riek think, Uhuru Kenyata will understand him better than the South Sudanese? Or does Riek want Kenya and IGAD countries to impose Federalism on South Sudan?

Now what is wrong with the current system of government or devolution in South Sudan?

When the Comprehensive Peace Agreement (CPA) was implemented in 2005, South Sudanese did not properly check the bag handed to them by the North. Their desperation for freedom or secession from the North blindfolded them. Even a new school with 8 classes is not filled at the same time but starts with enrollment of one class till reaching the capacity after eight years. The ten states and 79 counties inherited from Khartoum were not checked beforehand and compared to our economic power. At the implementation of the CPA, South Sudan accommodated at one ago over 400 political post holders in form of President, Vice President, National Ministers and Advisors, State Governors, state Ministers and Advisors, Chairpersons of Commissions at the national and state levels. That figure does not include over 700 honorable members in the 12 august houses of legislature, then, the hundreds of generals in the organized forces. All are catered for through the oil revenue. Then the militias were coming in and reversing at leisure but because of peace and reconciliation, all joined the ranks and files of our organized forces. All these expenses were covered through oil revenues, a source which was discovered in 1980 after 25 years of Torit Revolt and tapped in 1996 after 14 years of SPLM/A revolt. This means when South Sudanese thought of waging a liberation war, oil was not among the least potential resources. By the way the oil in South Sudan was discovered by a flying satellite in 1980 and Chevron, charlatans and vulture companies scrambled for the fortunes.

If we are honest with ourselves, the defunct regional government in the South laid a strong foundation to the successive systems of governments in the South. We know two essential elements are the backbone of any development, electricity and cement. The regional government brought in experts in those two fields and feasibility studies and researchers were carried out and Fula Rapids was found suitable for generating the hydroelectric power. On the other hand, Kapeota was found suitable for the production of cement.

Mangala area was feasibly fit for the production of Sugar cane. The area extending from Gumiza to northeast till Akobo is a very wide plain of land not less than 6 million hectares of fertile soil suitable for the growth of sugar cane, rice, sorghum and other food and cash crops. Then the largest mango forest in Western Equatoria, is the largest natural mango plantation in the world and if exploited could supply the whole of Africa of its needs from juice and slices. Then the livestock in their millions and fish from the crisscrossing streams and lakes that can suffice the local and export needs.

The government is like a football team and the head who is the president is the captain of that team. In other words, he is the first among equals. If a team is defeated in a match, it is not the captain who is to be blamed for the defeat it is the whole club including the managers and the couches. In the case of the government, the legislature, the political parties, the judiciary, the Auditor General and others are to be blamed. Even the drivers who overturn cars due to negligence or reckless driving are part and parcel of the inefficiency. Even again during a football match, players are changed from time to time. Not because the ones substituted are discarded or useless. Exactly that is the situation with a government.

Since establishment of the Government of South Sudan, many reshuffles took place. Most ministries have been reshuffled five to six times during the period. This means over 150 ministers and advisors have been removed and others brought in, in the national government alone. And definitely more than 700 Governors, advisors, state ministers and county commissioners have faced the same in the ten states of South Sudan. Among the few who survived the reshuffle since establishment of the Government of South Sudan till present, only four ministers and one state governor survived the continuous reshuffles, namely Michael Makuei Lueth, Awot Deng Acuil, Nunu Kumba, Dr. Barnaba Marial Benjamin and Governor Clement Wani Koanga of Central Equatoria.

Some of the reshuffled out lost elections in the last general elections but they were rewarded with ministerial positions for their failure.

When reshuffling was carried out in July 2013, the world got shaken but nobody gave himself a chance why was there no outcry when the previous reshuffles were done? Are the last reshuffled out better than Arthur Akuein, Dr. Anne Ito, Dr. Luka Manoja, David Deng Athorbei, Joseph Okel, Michael Milly Hussein, Kuol Athian, Alison Manani Magaya, Salva Mathok, James Kook Rue, Lual Acuil, Nhial Deng Nhial etc. If someone thinks the last reshuffled out are to be forced back into the government, all those reshuffled out since implementation of the CPA to independence should be reinstated.

If some are brandishing their glaring qualifications in the faces of South Sudanese, Please South Sudanese have many who obtained glaring qualifications some forty to fifty years ago; the kind of Dr. Francis Mading Deng, Dr. Akolde and many others but see how they have humbled themselves to serve under those younger in age and lesser in qualifications than them. They have humbled themselves. Our Lord Jesus Christ said: "Humble yourself and you will be exalted and exalt yourself and you will be humbled." I am afraid that those exalting themselves because of certain claimed qualities will regret in life one day. General Douglas Macarthur, the American hero in the Japanese and Korean war was fired by President Harry Truman, Field Marshal Zhukov, the most decorated Soviet Union general who defeated the Nazis in the Second World War was relegated by Stalin and Sergo Beria, the NKVD(Later KGB) boss was removed by Stalin.

[Still, why is the International Community silent about over 2000 innocent civilians massacred in a genocidal move in Bor by Riek Macar, Hussein Mar Nyuot, Gabriel Duop and Peter Gadet? Gadet is sanctioned for ordering themassacre of over 200 people in Bantiu but the one of Bor is ignored. The clear reason behind this is because Riek Macar will be involved and even UNMISS, a thing the sympathizers of Riek greatly fear and dread. When Riek ordered the massacre of Bor people, his command post was the VIP reception room in at Bor Airport.

The Archbishop of Canterbury witnessed the horrific massacre of Bor. It is UNMISS that revealed the massacre in Bentiu to the World.

Is UNMISS in Bentiu different from that in Bor? For the credibility of UN and Human rights bodies, the genocidal massacre that took place in Bor should be declared to the world.

Otherwise for Riek and associates to divert the attention of people of South Sudan to federalism and other petty issues is not the concern of the people of South Sudan at the moment]

One Dr. Riek Gai is struggling hard to save the lives of South Sudanese by treating people and vaccinating them while another Dr. Riek Macar is killing the same South Sudanese people with impunity. Please, Obama, Banki Moon, Hielda Johnston and IGAD Countries advice whom should the South Sudanese follow the healer or the killer?

Conclusion

To survive well and serve purpose of being a human we need at most discipline particularly self-discipline as it serves all of humankind and environment, we live in. Ecologically we need all creatures around us to be able to enjoy the world we are placed in by mighty creation. This means we need to respect and nurture the surrounding. To achieve this, we must possess the highest possible degree of self-discipline not re-enforce one. *"Honour your father and mother 'so that it may be well with you and you may live long on the earth'" (Ephesians 6:1–3)."*

Index

A

abilities and intelligence, 9
ability, 23, 27, 30
Acts Alliance, 46
ambush, 25, 61
Anglican Overseas, 45, 48, 50, 52, 54
appeal, 3, 45, 52, 53

B

believe, 23, 25
Bor, 6, 8, 10, 11, 13, 37, 38, 39, 40, 41, 42, 43, 45, 46, 47, 48, 49, 51, 53, 54, 55, 57, 62, 63, 65, 68, 69
Bor,, 10, 37, 39, 40, 46, 53
Brig. General Abraham Jongroor, 40

C

character, 14, 23, 29, 35, 58
Clement Wani, 67
ComprehensivePeace

Agreement, 65
conflict, 2, 24, 46, 48, 49, 50, 52, 53
culture, 2, 9, 12, 14, 29, 33, 36

D

December 2013, 37, 38, 54, 62
decisive, 15
discipline, vi, viii, ix, xiii, 2, 3, 4, 8, 14, 23, 24, 26, 27, 28, 30, 31, 32, 33, 35, 40, 57, 58
Discipline, 1, 3, viii, xiii, 2, 14, 23, 26, 27, 31, 32, 33, 34
disrespect, 2
Division 8, 39, 40, 41, 42
Douglas Macarthur, 68
Dr. Riek, 11, 24, 38, 65, 69

E

education, 3, 24, 29
Ethiopia, xii, 8, 13, 15, 17, 23, 25, 32, 43, 59
Ethiopian, 15, 16, 18, 24, 25, 32, 59

F

fighting, 3, 10, 11, 14, 24, 38, 41, 43, 45, 47, 53, 55
force, 10, 22, 23, 42, 52

G

Gadet, 39, 40, 41, 42, 68
goals, 2, 27, 31, 33
Got killed, 21
guns (Zu 23), the Soviet made, 19
Guolyar, 44, 45, 46, 49

I

I must stick, 16
Indiscipline, 4, 14, 57, 59, 60, 61
Internal Displaced Persons, 45

K

Kapeota, 66
Khartoum, 10, 11, 14, 21, 39, 58, 64, 65
killing, 10, 39, 42, 44, 64, 65, 69

L

leader, 10, 31, 39, 60
liability, 6
Liangary, 61

lifestyle, 12, 13, 32
loyalty, vi, 2, 30, 33, 34, 35
Lual Lual Akuei, 65
Luckily enough, 20

M

Maj. General Ajak Yen, 40
Maj. General Ajak Yen and Major General Tour Alier, 40
Malual Chaat, 41, 42, 43, 44
Mangala, 11, 66
Michael Makuei Lueth, 67
military Regime, 63

N

nature, 9, 57
negative forces, 36
nightmare, 19

P

Panpandiar, 40, 41, 42
participate, 58
patriarchal, 3, 5, 12
perseverance, 25
potential enemies of Islam, 18

Q

Quran teacher, 21

R

Rachel, xii, 44, 45, 56, 57
resilience, 4, 20, 23
responsibility, 2, 5
Riek Macar, 62, 63, 65, 68, 69
River Nile, 44, 46, 51

S

sacrifice, 8, 25
Self-discipline, xiii, 23, 26, 27, 29, 32
slaughtered, 10
Somalia, 3, 15, 18, 19, 20, 22
South Sudanese, 11, 28, 39, 48, 52, 54, 56, 60, 63, 64, 65, 68, 69
SPLA/M, 8, 9, 11, 24, 39, 58
SPLM/A, 10, 13, 14, 64, 66
stabber, 11
struggle, xi, 13, 25, 40, 58, 65

T

terrified, 42
tiny strip island, 17
tough, 4, 8, 15, 20
tribal behaviour, 39
truth, 31, 60

U

UNMISS, 68, 69

V

Vice President, 38, 48, 66
volunteering, 62

W

We are ambassadors, 29

www.ingramcontent.com/pod-product-compliance
Lightning Source LLC
Chambersburg PA
CBHW062043290426
44109CB00026B/2713